TESTIMON┃

"This book should be required for anyone going to college. It is invaluable information that all students need to know prior to enrolling."
—PAUL RAY, UTAH HOUSE OF REPRESENTATIVES

"Just using one of the techniques that Steven described has saved my wife and me almost $57,000 in college expenses—and that is just on one kid."
—CHARLES DOBENS, FOUNDER, MULTIFAMILY INVESTING ACADEMY

"[Steven] is loaded with proven strategies to lower college costs, get an excellent education, and graduate debt-free. Wow!"
—BRIAN TRACY, AUTHOR OF *GOALS!* AND PROFESSIONAL SPEAKER

"I found over $262,000 in money available for college because of what you taught."
—BRYCE, COLLEGE STUDENT, EVENT ATTENDEE

"Steven C. Roberts is a champion for reducing costs everywhere . . . on how to generate enough income in resourceful ways so that college loans are low or nonexistent."
—ANDY ANDREWS, BLOOMBERG BUSINESSWEEK

"My daughter just found over $411,000 in scholarships because of ONE principle you taught!"
—MOTHER OF HIGH SCHOOL STUDENT

"I couldn't put it down . . . I am just blown away by the power of that book! Not only a must-read for college students, but for EVERYONE!!!"
—CHRISTY RAY, TPR STORYTELLING, BLAINE RAY WORKSHOPS

"Just by applying a couple of the principles I learned from him within a few minutes, I was able to save just over $2,000 that same day! Steven has diligently done his research and thoroughly understands many concepts which other people don't fully comprehend . . . I feel that Steven is not only a wonderful writer, but he is also just as uniquely talented to be able to communicate in very understandable terms to many different age groups."
—BRAD, COLLEGE STUDENT

"This is the best 'how-to' book I have ever read about college. Very well done."
—JOHN PAUL CUTLER, STUDENT

"As part of my job as a high school counselor, I regularly advise students and help them prepare for college and point them to scholarships and other resources; I learned several new ideas and methods from Steven for helping the students I advise and even my own children. . . . After Steven spoke, several parents and students requested when they could hear him in other presentations. . . ."

—April Sagala, Jordan High School

"Who knew that a book on saving money could be so fun to read? Awesome job!"

—Justin Swalberg, MBA

"Steven did a wonderful job presenting his personal stories and concepts from his book in an engaging manner with a large audience. He really kept the attention of everyone in the audience. The information he presented was valuable and useful. The time really flew by and left you wanting more."

—Barbara, mother, event attendee

"[Steven's] presentation was so well-attended that we had standing room only! My staff heard dozens of comments about 'how great of an experience it was.' Steven is an effective and captivating presenter. We definitely would like to invite him back in the future!"

—Liesl Seborg, Senior Librarian, Salt Lake County Library

"Students are missing out on a goldmine of free money because they don't know where to find it or have no motivation to apply for it. Students are eligible for hundreds of scholarships they don't know about. . . . Roberts unveiled expert advice and techniques on how paying for college can be easier with the help of scholarships and grants."

—Jacob Amezcua, student, "Steven Roberts: How to pay for college without student loans," *The Daily Universe* (Brigham Young University, Provo, UT), April 13, 2015

Send Steven Your Results: *www.FindingCollegeCash.com/Feedback*

Some of the Principles Taught in this Book (there are lots more):

• Scholarships	• FAFSA	• Financial Counselors
• Grants	• Buying books	• Student loan dangers
• Getting a job	• Internship tips	• Tuition assistance
• Essay-writing	• Automating finances	• 5-Step Process

FREE GIFTS

Thank you so much for purchasing this book. There are two free gifts that I want to give you as a thank-you for your time and investment. These are tools to help you in your own quest to find and obtain money for college.

Gift One:
Get the workbook that goes with this book (valued at $25) for FREE. This will help you follow along and find money and resources for college.

Go to *www.FindingCollegeCash.com/FreeWB*

Gift Two:
Get a free video course to help you learn some ideas that can help you pay for college. The video course will help you learn some concepts to help with your education.

Go to *www.FindingCollegeCash.com/FreeVideo*

Thank you again for your commitment to your future, or the future of someone you care about. Many thanks for the trust you are placing in this book. I hope that it serves you well.

—Steven C. Roberts

C-A-S-H

The aim of this book is to help <u>YOU</u> get *C-A-S-H: Controlling expenses, Amplifying income, Set and achieve goals, and Have systems*™ for your life and for college. This book will help you find money for college, keep it, establish goals, and have systems to help you succeed.

This book is really **two books in one**. Part 1 teaches you to earn money for college. Part 2 teaches you how to keep your money and prevent debt in college—and long afterward.

The book is written as a story. Many of the principles you learn will help you in writing résumés, managing finances, and more. Topics can be found in the table of contents.

PROCESS TO GET MONEY FOR COLLEGE

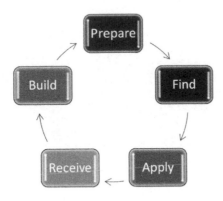

Some resources will have no or extremely low GPA requirements, other resources will have more competition. However, all of the resources will follow this pattern. If you find yourself stuck, you need to fix one of the steps. You will learn that there are more resources to pay for college than you may be aware exist. This book will teach you to use as many resources as you can, so that you can finish college debt-free or better! Right now, 70% of all college students get caught with debt that can last 10 to 30 years. **This book will show you multiple ways to pay for college**, so you can start your career, and next phases of life, free from student loans and other financial traps so many college students fall into.

FINDING COLLEGE CASH™

PROVEN IDEAS TO FIND SCHOLARSHIPS, GRANTS, AND OTHER

RESOURCES TO FINISH COLLEGE DEBT-FREE OR BETTER!™

STEVEN C. ROBERTS

WWW.FINDINGCOLLEGECASH.COM

ILLUMINATED ENTERPRISES, LLC

Illuminated Enterprises, LLC
391 E 1700 S #160131
Clearfield, UT 84015

Editions Available — First Edition 2018

Paperback
Kindle
PDF
EPUB

Editors: Liz Seif, Angela Ivey, Emily Grover
Typesetting and Layout: Sheenah Freitas
Cover Design: Maggie Wright, and Ari Gold
Photo credits: Commercial use photo purchased by Ari Gold

Publisher's Cataloging-in-Publication data
Names: Roberts, Steven C., author.
Title: Finding college cash : proven ideas to find scholarships , grants , and other resources to finish college debt-free or better! / Steven C. Roberts.
Description: Updated version of: Winning the Money Game in College | Includes bibliographical references. | Clearfield, UT: Illuminated Enterprises, LLC, 2017.
Identifiers: ISBN 978-0-9903147-4-5 (pbk.) | 978-0-9903147-5-2 (epub) | LCCN 2017914146
Subjects: LCSH College costs--United States. | Student aid--United States. | Education--United States--Finance. | Scholarships--United States. | Finance, Personal--United States. | BISAC STUDY AIDS / Financial Aid | EDUCATION / Finance | BUSINESS & ECONOMICS / Personal Finance / Money Management
Classification: LCC LB2342 .R61 2017 | DDC 378.3/8--dc23

This book is dedicated to Jana—my love and sweetheart.

*Jana my love, thank you for all of your support and encouragement—
not just with this book, but always.*

I love you.

This book is also dedicated to my children.

*You bring me such joy and happiness. Thank you for
being a part of my life.*

I love you.

Table of Contents

Foreword

The moment your first child is born, you begin to hear the almost daily mantra from other parents, "eighteen more years before you have to start writing big checks." Before you decide to sign on the dotted line and take out student loans for yourself or for your kids, note: student loans cannot be discharged in bankruptcy. Think about that for a moment. The federal government has made a deal with the issuers of student loans such that if the borrower gets into financial trouble, his mortgage may be discharged along with almost everything else, except student loans. Student loans take priority over most other forms of debt and, except in very rare circumstances, cannot be discharged. In many cases, these loans cannot be paid off early even if you have the money to do so. Those student loan companies must have great lobbyists.

So, before you start 'mortgaging' your future in the form of student loans, let's shift your paradigm. In this book, my friend Steven Roberts will take you on a journey. While the book is fictional in terms of the characters, the principles are true. What many people don't know about the book is that many of the principles and events Steven actually lived and practiced. He knows from firsthand experience that it is possible to pay for college without taking out student loans or hitting Mom and Dad up for money.

My wife and I have begun implementing many of the techniques that Steven lays out in this book. It is such a great feeling when you see the total cost of your child's college experience coming nowhere close to the 'retail' price that is advertised in the manuals found in every bookstore.

Is this book worth it? Just using one of the techniques that Steven described has saved my wife and me almost $57,000 in college expenses—and that is just on one kid. I have three more to go. If one can have that type of success as easily as we have, the answer is an emphatic yes, this book is worth GOLD.

Charles Dobens
Boston, MA

How to Use This Book

This is not a standard finance book—it is a story to teach principles. My hope is that you will enjoy reading this book and use the principles as you can see them implemented by the characters. *Finding College Cash* is written as a story and as an instructional guide. The book will read like a novel. As you follow Justin, a college freshman who learns two days before classes that he is completely on his own in paying for college, you will find the principles interwoven throughout the story. At the end of each chapter, the principles are outlined as tips and assignments, along with warnings and things to avoid.

As a suggestion, read through the story first—other readers have said that the story greatly helps them understand both what steps to take and how to implement them. After reading one chapter of the story, you can either read the end-of-chapter material or continue reading the entire story before going back and reviewing the tips, assignments, and warnings. Reading the end-of-chapter material may help to solidify your understanding and recall of the suggestions contained in the chapter. Also, the end-of-chapter material will allow you to quickly reference the suggestions contained in the chapter.

This book should be kept as a reference after you read it. For quick reference later, use the Table of Contents to find the principle you're interested in and then read the corresponding section or end-of-chapter material. Most of all, enjoy the book. It is written to engage both the right and left brain, as you will learn by reading the story and the practical advice that the story contains. This is a book that will help you learn about paying for college. You may soon forget you are reading a book on money and finance and simply enjoy the story.

Download the FREE Workbook to help you follow along and find cash for college. This will help you succeed on your own. Go to *www.FindingCollegeCash.com/FreeWB*

Chapter 1
A Rude Awakening

"What do you mean Dad can't keep his promise to pay for school?" a surprised Justin asked his mom on the phone.

"I know that this is hard to hear," she replied, "but we aren't going to be able to pay for your college expenses—including tuition—like we said we would."

"What happened? I mean, when I left home yesterday, Dad reassured me that he would pay for college and I didn't need to worry. What changed? Is Dad hurt?"

"No, he's fine physically, but this morning while you were at Grandma and Grandpa's house, his company gave him the option of either taking a 60% pay cut or being laid off. They explained that the company had been losing money, and he chose the pay cut. He came home early and told me. We're cutting every expense we can, and right now we simply can't meet other financial obligations and pay for your schooling."

"What are you going to do?" Justin asked, hoping that there was another solution to the problem.

"Dad is putting his résumé together and will stay on while he looks for a new job. I'm really sorry, honey, but we need to look out for our family and your brothers and sisters. We're not going to be able to help you with paying for college."

The news hit Justin as if he were being run over by a truck. This was really hard to take. Justin was not prepared for what his mom had said. His stomach sank. He hadn't planned on this and the news just made him feel sick.

Justin had left home in Saint George, Utah, the day before to attend Syracuse State University,[1] a state school. Before he left, his dad had reiterated the promise to pay for Justin's schooling. After staying overnight with his grandparents in Payson, Utah, to break up the trip, Justin had set off again. However, now, he was stuck at the side of the freeway with a flat tire, near the off-ramp for Springfield, Utah. Even without the flat tire, he was about three hours away from his final destination.

Planning to ask for an "advance" of some of his college expense money to help with the tire, Justin had called his mom. That was when he received the news: "We're not going to be able to keep our promise to pay for your college."

"What am I going to do? School starts in two days and if I don't get my prerequisites finished this semester, I won't be accepted for my major," Justin asked, pleading for a solution.

"Justin," his mom responded in a tone that only mothers possess. "You're 20 years old. You've been away from home before. You worked in Alaska as a tour guide bus driver. You worked in Mexico on a humanitarian service project. You provided for yourself both of those times. Find a way."

At these words, Justin thought of what his grandfather had told him just hours before, while staying at his house. As Justin was heading out for a run, he had found his grandpa reading. Seeing Justin, Grandpa had read aloud: "'For which of you, intending to build a tower, sitteth not down first, and counteth the cost, whether he have sufficient to finish it?'"[2] "Many of the world's problems," he added, "come from disregarding these two principles: taking a proper accounting of your money and living within your means.

"You're at an important time in your life, Justin. Learn everything you can about money and how it works. The habits you establish now will stay with you for the rest of your life."

---

1 Fictitious school name

2 Ratcliffe, Susan. "Foresight." In Oxford Treasury of Sayings and Quotations, 175. Oxford: Oxford University Press, 2011. See also, Luke 14:28, KJV.

Justin now felt he'd been handed a heavy burden as he realized that he was completely unprepared to pay for college. Grandpa's advice now felt like condemnation for his lack of preparation. At the time, it had just seemed like unsought advice from an old man that Justin would soon forget, but now he felt bitter about the situation and angry with his dad's company. However, Justin heard himself say: "It'll be fine, Mom. I can find a way. I'll get a student loan or something."

"Make wise decisions, honey. We love you."

"I'll try to, and I love you too," Justin said. He had the sense not to mention the flat tire again.

"You might want to call Dave and Susan and tell them you're going to be late," his mother reminded him.

Justin's older cousin Dave and his wife Susan had agreed to let him stay at their home a few miles from school for a week or until he found a place to stay—whichever came first.

"'Kay, I'll give them a call."

"Wherever you go to get your tire fixed, ask if they have discounts for students—remember to get the price first, then ask for the discount in order to prevent being bid up."

"Thanks," Justin said dispiritedly. They said their goodbyes and he went to work on changing the tire.

For a long time, Justin's dad had promised to pay for schooling, and when he had left home the day before Justin had felt that his life was just about perfect. Being accepted to SSU, taking the prerequisites offered in the fall semester, his dad paying for schooling costs, living at his cousin's house for a week—Justin had thought, *I've got it made.*

What had sealed the deal for going to SSU was finding out his good friend Paul was already there. Paul had told Justin about SSU and told him he could find a place to rent on the student housing board in the student center. Paul and Justin had made plans to hang out—starting with going to a dance two days before classes were to begin. Instead, Justin was at the side of the freeway changing a flat tire, the dance was supposed to start in a few hours, and Justin had no idea how to pay for school. *What am I going to do? I should tell Paul I'm going to be late. He's waiting for me.*

Moment of Decision and Taking Action

Justin called his cousin Dave, but got only his voicemail. He left a message about the tire and said he would call back. Justin started to put his spare tire on, his mind racing with thoughts about possible options for paying for school. *If I don't start this semester, I won't get my prereq's done and I won't be able to be accepted into my major.* <u>*I don't care how … I am going to still go to school. I will find a way.*</u> *I want to be accepted by my major. I've got about $1,000 in my bank account—maybe I can get a student loan for the rest. Perhaps I can meet with a representative from a bank. How do other people going to college get scholarships? Are there options for me, or just the privileged few? Why did Dad's work have to go and do a thing like that? I guess I will just do what everyone else does. I mean, I can always pay it off after I graduate, right?*

Once the spare was in place, he pulled out his phone again. This time he searched for a tire store. An app gave him directions, and he was soon on his way to buy a new tire.

Ask for a Discount

Upon entering the store, Justin announced to a store clerk, "I have a flat tire. What would it cost to get it replaced including parts, labor, and all fees, as the final cost?" After getting some vehicle information, the clerk gave him a quote.

Remembering the conversation with his mom, Justin asked, "Do you have any specials or discounts for students?"

"We do have a discount for students, 10% off," replied the man. "Do you have your student ID?"

"I'm a freshman, my car is packed and I'm headed up to Syracuse State University; I don't have a student ID yet."

After a bit of consideration, the salesman replied, "I'd be willing to give you 10% off without your ID."

"That sounds great," Justin said, disgruntled about the flat tire but happy to get a discount.

"There's a bit of a wait, so we won't be able to get to this for another thirty to forty minutes. People always seem to wait until the end of the day to come in," warned the clerk.

"Good to know. After the wait, how long will it take to change the tire?" Justin asked hopefully.

"About thirty minutes."

There was no guarantee that if he went to a new store, he would get a discount. Additionally, considering how close it was to closing time, he might not get serviced today.

"Well, let's get started," Justin said. "My car is the green Toyota Tercel." He handed the clerk his keys.

He took a seat in the waiting area, still pondering his new dilemma. While he waited, he tried calling his cousin again. Dave's phone rang three times, and just as Justin thought he would have to leave another voicemail, he heard a hurried "Hello!"

"Hi, Dave, this is Justin."

"Hey, how's it going?" asked his older cousin. "I got your message. Were you able to get your tire taken care of?"

"Well, I was able to get the spare put on, and I'm at a tire store now. The clerk said that it would take over an hour, due to the last-minute rush," Justin responded.

"That should put you here at about 8:30 or 9:00, assuming all goes well, right?" asked Dave. After he agreed, his cousin added, "Well, be safe. When you get here, I'll help you unload and show you where you can sleep."

"Okay, thanks," said Justin. "Hey, Dave ..." Justin began.

"Yeah?"

"How'd you pay for college? I mean I was just wondering how to make ends meet," Justin said, not wanting to mention his dad's pay cut to his cousin.

"Well, I was able to get a student loan and that saw me through school. If you need to, you can meet with a school counselor who specializes in student loans. College can be rough financially, but it may help you earn a higher income."

"Thanks for the info, bye," Justin said.

Justin felt deflated by his cousin's words. He was now also worried about the time. *It'll be nine o'clock when I get there? I don't know if I'm going to make it to this dance*, Justin thought. I'd better call Paul.

"Justin! Are you in Syracuse?" asked Paul excitedly as he answered the phone.

"Well, actually, my car had a flat tire. Now I'm in a tire store in a small town called Springville."

Paul responded, "That's about three hours away. How are you planning on making it to the dance?"

"Um, *I* was wondering that as well," Justin said in a slightly disappointed tone. It wasn't so much the dance that he was interested in—it was seeing Paul again. "The tire guy said that it would be just under an hour before my car would be finished," continued Justin.

"Okay…well, maybe we can do *something* when you get in," said Paul. "The dance goes until 10:00."

"I'll call you when I get to Syracuse, but don't count on it being early enough to go the dance," replied Justin.

"Well, that's no fun," Paul pouted jokingly. "Take care, though. Oh—and don't rush it; I-15 has a couple of speed traps. I wouldn't push it too much," Paul cautioned.

"Thanks for the warning," said Justin.

"Don't worry," continued Paul. "This dance isn't the only thing to do at SSU. We'll still have lots of time to hang out and do stuff together."

Justin wondered if he should tell Paul about his dad's pay cut and his sudden lack of funds—this would severely limit his fun.

"Hey, do you know how to get a student loan?" Justin asked, trying not to sound too obvious or desperate.

"Wait, why do you care? Isn't your dad going to pay for your college anyway? Student loans are for the rest of us who don't have it made," Paul said with a hint of curiosity.

"Dad's work had him take a 60% pay cut instead of a layoff. Now my parents can't afford to pay for my school."

"*Ewllll*...Dude, that stinks!" Paul said.

"Tell me about it," Justin replied. "I am still coming to school, but now I need to come up with funds soon."

"We can make it happen; you can get a student loan and maybe I might be able to help you learn some ways to save some money," Paul said. "We can still have a lot of fun together."

"We'd better," said Justin jokingly. "Take care."

"See ya' man," Paul replied.

Avoid Unnecessary Expenses

Justin soon regretted not grabbing some of the snacks his grandma had given him before turning his keys over. He looked around the store for vending machines. In the corner, he saw some small candy dispensers full of chalky chocolate candies. Not appetizing. Justin looked out the window and saw a fast-food place. He thought about going there.

Hmmm, a couple of tacos and some enchiladas, he thought. *This could be good.* He walked towards the front of the tire store. But then he realized that he didn't want to blow any money when he already had food available—especially now that he was paying for school. He went back to the same man who had helped him when he came into the store.

"It will be about another ten minutes before we get to your car," the man said before Justin could say anything.

"Thanks," Justin said, as friendly as he could be, considering the wait ahead. "I just wanted to have my keys so that I could get some food from my car."

"Sure thing," replied the man as he grabbed Justin's keys and then tossed them to him. "Just have them back soon so I can give them to the mechanic."

"Thanks," said Justin. He went out and unlocked his car door. After rummaging through his care package from his grandma, he grabbed some fruit and crackers and a water bottle. He re-locked his car and knocked on the door of the store to be let back inside. He handed the keys back to the man.

Sitting down again, Justin started fiddling with his smartphone. After eating more of his quick meal, he felt a lot better.

The TV in the lobby was tuned to a news station, and a brief segment came on about college. At the mention of the words "money" and "college," the story had Justin's attention.

The news reporter was talking about how student loan debt had reached $1.38 trillion, with recent graduates in 2016 averaging $37,172 and more than seven million borrowers defaulting, partly because many students used the student loan money to party.[3] About 27% of students who borrowed,[4] couldn't make the payments for one reason or another and then ended up in serious financial trouble. The reporter said something that really hit home for Justin:

> *A lot of students gamble, going to college and think that taking out a student loan will help them have a better life, but what many of them don't realize is that having a degree does not guarantee them a higher paying job—or any job at all. Many students falling victim to this*

---

3   "US Student Loan Debt Clock & Statistics, and Facts 2017." Debt Clock. Accessed March 1, 2017. https://debtclock.tv/world/us/student-loan/

4   "With Student Loans Equal to All Income Tax Collection, 27% Are in Defaults." Breitbart. Accessed August 9, 2017. http://www.breitbart.com/big-government/2015/04/15/study-over-27-of-student-loans-are-in-default/

mentality go into majors that are not in demand or attend expensive schools, and then after they finish school, reality hits hard. And unfortunately, as the Washington Post reported, many students who attend certain for-profit schools find that they make less after attending these institutions than they did without the degree[5] and that some schools often encourage their students to get more student loan debt.

The reporter went on to talk about how student loan debt has drastically increased over the last 10 years and many students find out too late that the loans are often inescapable because they usually cannot be wiped out through bankruptcy when a crisis hits. *"Another problem,"* the reporter continued, *"is that even if students can find a job, they are often shocked at how much debt they have and just how high the payments are. The average student loan debt is over $37,000 per student for a four-year degree. Now, remember, that is not for doctors or lawyers. That is just a bachelor's degree. That is the average, and many students end up with hundreds of thousands in student loan debt. Sadly, many students find the bill is too high."*

Justin went numb. He had believed, and even told his mom, that he would get a student loan. A heavy, gloomy feeling descended on him. *I am NOT going to end up in debt,* he thought.

The clerk interrupted Justin's thoughts and said, "Your car's ready to go. I can ring you up at the register." Justin followed the man over to the register and was given his invoice. "Your total is $76.73 with the discount," said the man. Justin paid and soon enough he was back on the road.

The rest of the trip passed without incident. Justin arrived in Syracuse

---

5   The Washington Post. "A popular college investment promised students a career, but didn't pay off." Accessed April 12, 2017. https://www.washingtonpost.com/news/wonk/wp/2016/05/31/a-popular-college-investment-promised-students-a-career-but-didnt-pay-off

a little after 9:20 p.m. and drove to Dave's. He was welcomed and shown where he could sleep. He brought some of his bags in. By this time it was after 10:15 so Justin called Paul and said he didn't feel up to getting together this late. Paul was disappointed, but he understood. Justin got ready for bed. He was tired after traveling all day and fell right to sleep.

Chapter 1: Principles and Suggestions

1. With planning, work, resourcefulness, and commitment, anyone can attend college and finish without debt.

2. Creating a plan for your education can help you. A major not in demand may not be the best choice. Just because you like art that does not mean that you need to be a sketch artist. You can also be a business major, computer graphics major, advertising and marketing major, teacher, accountant, etc.

3. Going to the right type of school can be very important. The Washington Post reports that students who went to some for-profit schools earned less after college than before and were not adequately prepared for a career.[6] (See Workbook.)

4. Justin's grandpa was correct: Most financial problems occur when people don't take an accounting of their finances and live within their means. What are some ways that you can measure where you stand financially? What are some ways to live within your means?

---

6   The Washington Post. "A popular college investment promised students a career, but didn't pay off." Accessed August 9, 2017. https://www.washingtonpost.com/news/wonk/wp/2016/05/31/a-popular-college-investment-promised-students-a-career-but-didnt-pay-off

Chapter 1: Assignments

Get the free workbook at *www.FindingCollegeCash.com/FreeWB*

1. Complete the "Why Do I Want to Go to College?" activity in the workbook. This can help you focus your purpose and goals.

2. Complete the "Choose a Major that Can Pay" in the workbook.

3. Start researching ways to save money and pay for college.

4. Complete the "My Total College Costs" worksheet.

5. Complete the "Picking a College" section in the workbook.

6. Practice asking for discounts. It can be intimidating, but students, especially, often qualify for good discounts.

Chapter 1: Warnings and What to Avoid

1. Will Rogers is often quoted as saying: "Too many people spend money they haven't earned to buy things they don't want, to impress people they don't like."[7] Avoid being like that.

2. Justin stopped himself from buying unneeded restaurant food. Spending money a little here and there is what is referred to as being a *bubblegum-diamond thief*[TM], which is someone who trades small, insignificant expenses for what you really want. If you spend too much money, you will end up in debt.

---

7 Rogers, Will. "Will Rogers Quotes." BrainyQuote. Accessed August 15, 2017. https://www.brainyquote.com/quotes/will_rogers_167212.

Chapter 2
Decisions to Reduce Costs

After his run the next morning, Justin hit the kitchen for breakfast. Dave came in, looking a little sleepy. "How's it going?" he asked as he rubbed his eyes. "I have to get to work, but I would recommend, Justin, that you head over to the campus to see if you can find a job and get your student ID. I hear jobs on campus and in surrounding areas go quickly."

"Thanks," said Justin. "I was going to go get my student ID then look for a job. I have an appointment at 11:00 to see a school counselor to add my final classes."

"A counselor for *classes*?" Dave asked inquisitively.

"That's right," replied Justin.

"Man, you are brave," said Dave. "When I was a student there, all of the fun classes were gone by the day before classes started."

"*Fun* classes?" Justin asked.

"Yeah, you know, the ones that make college bearable—things like volleyball, golf, and karate," said Dave.

"I guess I was focusing too much on the classes for my major," Justin responded. "I hadn't really thought about adding any *fun* classes to my schedule."

"Well, you'd better," emphasized Dave. "Do you have a plan for getting a student loan?"

"I'll try to get an appointment later today."

"Well, good luck. At least you are going to an in-state school to reduce tuition costs and fees."

"Thanks," Justin said as he started to feel a little overwhelmed with all he had to do.

Justin, Dave, and Susan ate and then went their separate ways. When Justin got to campus, he asked around and got directions to the Student Center building. As he walked to it, he observed how beautiful the campus was, with its old trees and well-planned landscaping. The buildings were similar to each other in design and had the same style of bricks. In addition to being well kept, the campus was also very busy; students and faculty members were making last-minute preparations for the start of classes the next day.

As Justin neared the Student Center, he noticed the building was already crowded with people busily moving around. He made his way to the front desk.

"I'm new here. Where do I go to get my student ID?" Justin asked a girl who stood behind the counter.

"Go down this hall and make a left. The ID Center is the second door on the right," the girl replied automatically.

Justin thanked her and went on his way toward the ID Center. As Justin turned the corner, he saw a line extending out of the second door on the right.

In spite of what seemed like thirty people in front of him, the line moved quickly, and in less than ten minutes, Justin was at the counter. After his photo was taken, he was handed his student ID.

As he left the ID Center, his phone rang. It was Paul. Justin stepped away from the crowd to take the call.

"We missed you last night, man," were Paul's first words when Justin answered his phone.

"I know. Getting a flat tire on a trip has got to be on the list of least favorite traveling experiences."

"So where *are* you?"

"I'm in the Student Center. I just got my student ID," Justin said.

"You're on campus! Sweet! So am I," was the reply. "Before you go to the bookstore, I have to show you something. Come meet me at the library. It will be well worth it to you, *financially* I mean," Paul said with emphasis.

"Okay. Where is the library?" Justin asked, feeling lost already.

"It's the building to the south of the Student Center. I'll meet you in the library lobby," replied Paul.

"Okay, I should be there in a few minutes," Justin said as he started walking south.

Justin had met Paul while on his humanitarian service project in Mexico. They were both from Utah and had hit it off. Paul was about a year older than Justin and had been in Mexico longer, so he had helped Justin to learn some of the more vital phrases in Spanish: *¿A qué hora viene el autobús?* (When does the bus come?), *¿Dondé está el baño?* (Where's the bathroom?), and *¡¿Qué pasa, calabaza?!* (A fun phrase: What's happening dude/pumpkin/pumpkin head?).

Paul had also been the source of some discomfort during Justin's first week in Mexico. The local women would occasionally provide meals for the volunteers, and Paul had told Justin that it was offensive to say no to more food. He had said that the polite way to decline additional helpings was to say "*Cómo no*" when offered more food. It wasn't until after his fourth helping of *sopa de pollo y arroz* (chicken and rice soup) that Justin had realized that it was a setup: '*¿Cómo no?*' means "Sure, why not?" Paul had thought his joke was hilarious, as Justin grabbed his bowl and covered it to prevent his being given fifths that night.

"Dude!" said Paul in the library lobby upon seeing Justin again.

"Hey, old man!" said Justin with a smile.

"Good to see ya', man," Paul said warmly.

"It's good to see *you*," said Justin as he gave Paul a quick hug.

"As you can see," said Paul, "the library is busy."

And it was. Justin had noticed people sitting at computers in the library's computer terminal section.

"This library has *talking* sections and *quiet* sections," Paul continued. "When I heard you were on campus, I grabbed us two computers in the talking section. We need to get back there soon so no one moves my stuff," Paul said, pointing to the area.

They walked quickly to the section Paul had indicated. On their way, Paul asked, "Did you have a good drive—minus the tire?"

"Yeah," replied Justin. "I was able to see my grandparents on my mom's side."

Paul suddenly stopped at a large desk with a sign that read "Computer Help" on it.

"You have your student ID, right?"

"Just got it!" replied Justin with enthusiasm because he realized he was officially a student now.

"Excuse me," said Paul, turning to the attendant who was sitting at a computer, reading a book. The attendant looked up. "My friend here is a freshman on campus and would like to have access to the computer network."

"May I see your student ID?" the guy asked.

Justin handed it over.

The attendant swiped the ID card and handed it back, asking Justin what he wanted his username to be. After typing some other identifying information into the computer, the attendant passed Justin the computer keyboard and asked him to type in a password. Justin did so and returned the keyboard.

"This is some job you've got here," Paul said.

"I know," said the attendant. "That should do it," he said to Justin. "You'll need to wait about 10 minutes before logging onto the network. You can log into the school's website with your username and password," he added.

Paul and Justin hurried to where their computers were waiting; he'd reserved them by putting his bag near them. "Glad no one took my stuff," Paul said as he sat down.

Method for Buying Discounted Text Books

"First things first," Paul said. "Let's get you some books. I told you that meeting up would be financially rewarding, and it's time to make good on my promise—starting with books. The school is pretty good about putting each class book list online. But they wait until two days before school starts to release it publicly."

"I haven't finished signing up for all my classes yet," Justin said.

"That's fine," said Paul. "We'll start with what you have." Paul directed the computer's web browser to the school website and clicked the "Sign In" link. He handed the keyboard over to Justin to type in his own username and password. Paul then went to Justin's profile and showed him how to access his book list, a web-generated form that had a list of book titles, editions, authors, and ISBNs.

"Hmm, it looks like for your current class schedule, you need to get eleven books," said Paul. "It appears that you still need to register for two more credit hours to be a full-time student." Paul pointed to the book list.

"How convenient," said Paul in a semi-sarcastic tone. "They list the prices in the bookstore so you can see how much you'll have to shell out. It looks like your most expensive book is $122.99."

Justin couldn't believe it. The books totaled over $600. Paul must have seen the look on Justin's face as he saw the total price. "Scary, isn't it?" asked Paul in a reassuring tone. "Now, let Paul the magician do his magic and show you how to beat the system."

"Okay," said Justin.

"Normally, I decide which classes I'm absolutely going to take the next semester and then email each teacher, weeks in advance, saying that I am enrolled in his or her class and asking what the book titles, authors, and ISBNs are, and which books are *required* and which are *optional*. I order the books from eBay or Amazon, and use Bigwords as a search engine. They get here in plenty of time. In your case, we're going to do this with a slight twist."

"What do you mean?" asked Justin. "School starts tomorrow; I can't pay for overnight shipping just to get a book here."

"Well," said Paul, "in your case, considering that $122.99 book on the list, overnight shipping would still be a cheaper solution than the bookstore prices."

"Are you serious?" Justin asked, surprised.

"Think about it," responded Paul. "Say we can get the book for $85 online, and it costs $30 to overnight the book to you. What is the sum of $85 + $30?" Paul asked.

"That's $115," Justin replied, realizing that the bookstore price would be $122.99, plus tax.

"Now are you beginning to see?" asked Paul. "But I think we can do *better* than an eight-dollar savings."

Paul's words really piqued Justin's interest. "Okay," he said, "now you've got me listening. How do you do *that*?"

"Well, we happen to be in a library. Unfortunately, we're a little late. Like I mentioned, I typically have all my books shipped to me weeks in advance, but we'll see what we can do. Let's look at the online library catalog and see if there are any books *here* that you need," Paul continued.

"And I just renew them out from the library each week! Brilliant!" Justin said excitedly as he interrupted.

"Um, no," Paul said in a polite but correcting tone. "Lots of freshmen try to do that, but the library has policies against multiple renewals of the same book. Even if they didn't, there's at least one other student who has the same idea. You end up either not being able to renew your book when you need it—say, right about midterms—or you get in a check-out war of who gets it. In the end, it costs you time, as well as money in library fines because you don't want to return the book for fear that you won't have it when you need it. You can ask me how I know *that* one.

"The only exception," Paul continued, "is if the teacher reserves a copy at the library service desk, you can borrow the book for a few hours to read.

Speaking from experience, that's a good option if you just need to read the book for homework."

Justin could tell that Paul knew some of the ins and outs of this college thing, especially when it came to buying books. That was one of the things that he liked about Paul, his attention to detail.

"Okay, professor, teach me," Justin said with a smile.

"We check out the books just long enough for the online shipments to get here," Paul said with a wry smile. "The post office's Media Mail option is a good one because it reduces shipping costs, and packages can typically get here before you have to return the book."

"*Nice*," Justin said in awe, realizing he was learning from both a friend and a master of the system.

Three of Justin's books were available at the library, with one more already checked out that was due back in two weeks. Paul helped Justin place holds on all four books. "We'll grab the three books that are in today before you leave," Paul assured Justin. "Next, we need to find the books online. Let's start at ebay.com and amazon.com with your book list."

They copied the ISBN codes into the search fields. To save time, they opened the search results showing books they wanted to know more about in new tabs in an internet browser. By this time, Justin was able to log onto a computer, which sped up the search.

"Here's a good one," Justin said as he was searching. "It's only about 30% of the bookstore cost."

"Whoa!" said Paul. "'Danger, Will Robinson!'" he quoted with a grin.

"What do you mean?" Justin asked, a bit confused.

"Because it's so close to the start of a semester," said Paul, "and because your book is a newer edition, most books online go up in price. If your book is that cheap, be sure to check to see if it's the *international version* of the book. The international version can be—not always, but can be—a knockoff version that usually someone in a foreign country paid to have copied by some low-paid worker. The wording, pages, page numbers, graphs, and pictures often are skewed, stuff can be missing, or just wrong, and usually they're black and white, instead of in color like the original. The ink color is not so much a problem for books that are strictly text, but when it comes to pictures and graphs, you'll wish you could see what's being described. Also, they're harder to sell, or resell."

Paul continued, "I know that's a lot of info, but it's important to know what you're getting before you buy it. I've found it's just not honest, either. First, the company that copied the book may not have permission from the publisher, and second, the sellers dishonestly try to represent the book as the real deal. That's why you should always check the book description from the seller. When in doubt, you can message the seller and ask. On the bright side, if the seller doesn't disclose this, most online companies like eBay or Amazon will refund the money and protect the buyer."

"Good to know," Justin said.

Sure enough, the book was the international edition. Justin skipped that one. After finding all of the books online, Justin was curious about why they hadn't bought any yet. Finally, he asked Paul about it.

"Well, we've spent a total of about fifteen minutes searching. We'll add the best-quality books in your price range to your shopping cart, and they're usually reserved for about fifteen minutes so that you won't lose them to another buyer. If we stopped here, you would be in good shape. But let's check two more spots. There's a student book exchange here at SSU. Let's look and see if any of your textbooks are there."

Justin first added the other books to his online shopping cart and then gave Paul the keyboard to direct his browser to the online book exchange. After Paul did so, Justin quickly copied and pasted the ISBNs to the search field of the web page. Three of his books were available. One was about $2.50 more than the web prices that Justin had previously found, with the other two being close to the bookstore prices.

"You should get the book that's $2.50 more," said Paul.

"Why?" asked Justin, confused as to why his friend was suggesting paying *more* for a book when he thought he was trying to save money.

"The reason," Paul continued, "is that *this* book you can get *now*. If you add up the shipping, you're just about there, but this book you can physically *see*, and if you don't like it, you can go back to the online books. Remember, 'A bird in hand is worth two in the bush.'"

Justin called the seller and made arrangements to see the book in about an hour. Ironically, the seller suggested that they meet in a building near the library; Paul gave directions.

"Okay," said Justin to Paul, "you mentioned there are *two* additional spots to check. Where is the second?"

"Before we go on, let's finish the first," Paul said.

Paul directed Justin to bigwords.com and did some searches for some of the books. After finding one of the books, Paul said it was time to go to the second method.

"Last, we look for digital versions of the book," he explained. "Some students are passionate about *real* books and others like the convenience of carrying most of their books with them on their smartphone or tablet. You won't really know which you prefer until you try both. I'd recommend trying a digital book that's mostly text, and see if you like it. Most of the time digital books are cheaper than physical books, but they can't be resold, so only buy the book digitally if you can't get it cheaper as a physical copy or if you wouldn't mind keeping a digital copy for yourself. Typically, I only use digital books that are under $30.00."

"How do I find a digital copy?" Justin asked.

"Go back to eBay or Amazon where we found your books and open a new tab to a link that says something like 'Other Editions.' That's where you find them if they exist."

Getting Paid for Buying Textbooks

Justin followed the instructions and found five of his books had other editions. Three of the five were old editions, one was a digital edition, and the last was a new edition that was a newer revision than what his book list required. The newer edition also happened to be one of the books that Justin had reserved at the library.

"Goldmine!" said Paul excitedly.

"What's a gold mine?" Justin asked.

"Look," responded Paul, "if you find a book that the campus is using repeatedly in the older edition, you can order, like, five to six extra copies every semester and sell them for five or ten dollars less than the used-book price offered at the bookstore by posting an ad on the book exchange or by going early to class and writing your ad on the chalkboard. The trick is to e-mail the teacher each semester and ask what books are required so that you don't get stuck with the extra books you might buy. I did this with a book that I could get for $7 online, and I sold it for $58 to other students, since the professors continued to use the old edition. The students were happy to get a book for $10 less than the bookstore price, and I helped the class have ample books—*plus,* I made about $50 per book that I sold![8] I did this for three semesters, selling about four books a semester. I did get stuck with two unsold books one semester because I had over-ordered and hadn't marketed enough before the campus finally updated the edition they used. But I listed and sold the two older edition books *at cost* on the book exchange, specifically mentioning that the books were the former editions, so I suffered no loss. Over three semesters, I made about $500 dollars, and I only wish I had bought more books when I first knew about it."

"So, wait," said Justin. "You buy extra books every semester and sell them to other students?"

"Well, yeah, why not? I help the students, and I help myself. A few weeks in advance of the new semester, I just email the professors of the classes I'm going to take, find cheap copies of the books, get them shipped to me, and then advertise like crazy the week before and the week after

8   The author really did this for multiple semesters, profiting greatly.

classes start—trying to get students to buy my books by posting on the book exchange and in classrooms directly. You'd be surprised how many students wait until the last minute to get books." Paul carefully didn't say "like you."

"I really do the same amount of work as I would have done for myself; I just add some additional books to my order. I usually get all of my books paid for this way, plus I earn a little extra money for each semester," Paul said with a hint of excitement in his voice.

"That is so awesome," Justin said.

"I know," Paul responded. "Just don't tell everyone my secrets. I'm telling *you* because you're my friend, and I think you need to learn the ropes of saving money on books. Plus, I was sorry to hear about your dad and your lack of funds. You may not be able to sell any books *this* semester, but keep it in mind for later. Now that you know most of my tricks for finding cheaper books, don't make the same mistakes I made and pay inflated book prices."

"Okay," Justin responded.

After placing his orders for his online books and for a digital book that was $10, he still had to buy a campus-published workbook that was $13.99. His total was $233.47. "Wow! I saved about $360 from what I would have spent when I was at the Student Center," Justin remarked.

"I'll take a check for my commission," said Paul jokingly. "But seriously, a few hundred dollars every semester makes a big difference. I *told you* meeting with me would be worth your time."

"Thanks for your help! The past half-hour or so has saved me a lot of money." Justin was relieved.

"You're welcome," said Paul. "And don't worry. Soon, you'll be able to do what we did today in just about ten minutes. I haven't told you everything, but I'm sure you can figure out some more of this on your own. Find what's honest and works and then use it to your advantage."

Paul looked at the time. "Hey, listen, I need to go meet up with my girlfriend Anna. Just be sure to get the library copies of the textbooks before you go. You'll want to get those soon so that they aren't taken by other students."

"I'll get right on it," Justin said. "Besides, I have to go meet the guy I called about selling me his book."

"A few last pieces of advice," Paul said.

"What are those?" Justin asked.

Knowing Your Options

"First, in spite of what you may think, you may not even need a student loan. Many students think that they need a student loan, but there are alternatives. For example, the university offers a low-interest payment plan for students who can pay the full amount of tuition for the semester by the end of the semester. You can pay some money upfront, and then pay the rest over the semester if you can get a job. While it's better to pay the full amount upfront to avoid any interest, this plan helps avoid some of the costs of student loans. Check with the tuition office to see if that's an option that could work for you.

"Second, if you do end up absolutely needing a student loan, check with multiple places because different organizations have different rates, fees, and payment schedules. I'd recommend checking with the campus financial aid office and your bank, and then comparing at least those two options."

"Thanks for the heads up," Justin said.

"Sure thing," Paul replied. "Hey, you should come by my place for a movie tonight."

"What time?" Justin asked.

"Seven o'clock. We'll have a small party," Paul replied.

"Sounds fun," Justin said.

"If you still haven't found a place to live by the time you need to leave your cousin's place, I'll beg my landlord to let you share rooms with me at my apartment," Paul added.

Paul gave Justin his address and left. Justin recorded his expenses in his smartphone and then went to the librarian's desk and asked how to find the books he had placed on hold. This was by far the biggest library he had ever seen, with literally miles of rows of books on multiple floors. The librarian gave Justin a map and showed him how to find the books he needed. He spent the next thirty minutes wandering the aisles. After getting turned around a few times, Justin found his books.

He left the library to meet the seller from the book exchange. He still had a meeting with a counselor at one o'clock, but at least he had most of his books, either with him or on order.

*...3148, 3150, 3154...*Justin thought as he passed rooms in the building's hallway. He was looking for room 3206 where the seller had said to meet him. Justin hoped that after meeting with the school counselor, he would have time to locate the rooms where his classes were, as well as find a job and try to get a student loan. He passed rooms 3200, 3202, 3208. *Hey, wait, where are 3204 and 3206?* He was at a hallway intersection, confused. Then he saw a large glass office with the words "Campus I.T. Resources" printed on the glass. The door was open, so he decided to check with someone inside.

Types of Jobs to Get

"Hi. I'm looking for room 3206, and I was wondering if you could tell me where to go," Justin said to a cute girl behind the reception desk, who was obviously the secretary.

"You're here," was the reply. "The I.T. office is part of rooms 3204 and 3206."

"I called about a book from the book exchange, and a guy named Dan told me to meet him in 3206," Justin said.

"Hold on," the secretary said. She punched in an extension on the telephone, and Justin heard a ring in one of the cubicles in the office. The secretary spoke into the phone. "Dan, there's a guy here saying that you posted a book on the book exchange and that you told him to meet you here." Justin could faintly hear a male voice somewhere in the office. "Uh huh, okay. I'll send him over." She hung up the phone and smiled at Justin. "Just go to the fourth row over there, and go six cubes back," she said, pointing.

Justin thanked her and followed her directions, stopping at a cubicle that had "Daniel" written on a nameplate. The cubicle was an open one that shared space with an adjacent one. Two guys just a little older than Justin were seated on opposite walls.

"Are you Dan?" Justin said, hoping one of them would answer.

"I'm Jon," was the first reply.

"I'm Dan," replied the guy to Justin's left. "Are you here about the book?"

"Yeah," Justin said.

"Here it is," Dan responded, holding up his copy.

The book's cover was slightly worn, so Justin asked if he could browse through it. Dan agreed that he could.

As Justin was looking at the book, an older gentleman hurriedly came in and addressed Jon. "Jon, did you hear that Stewart said he couldn't work this semester because he was accepted as a biology TA? We need to quickly find someone to take his place and work his shift at the MK building."

"Do you want me to call Student Services and post the job?" asked Jon.

At the mention of the word "job," Justin's attention turned to the conversation next to him.

"Do you think we can get someone to cover for him until we get a replacement?" Justin heard Jon say to the older man.

"Excuse me," said Justin, turning to face them. "I couldn't help overhearing. Did you say that you need to find someone to cover a shift? I'm looking for a job. What position are you talking about?"

The older man turned to him. "Computer lab monitor."

"A what...?" Justin asked.

"Have you seen the computer help desks or information desks at the library?" asked the man.

"Yes. I was helped there earlier this morning," replied Justin.

"Well, there are computer labs all over campus," said the man, "and we need to have someone in each lab to help people with their computers, word processing, and internet access. The people in the labs are called computer lab monitors. If there is no lab monitor, campus policy requires us to close the computer lab. We need to find someone to cover the computer lab at the MK Building between 2:30 and 6:00 in the afternoon, Monday through Friday. What experience do you have with computers?"

Justin wasn't sure where the MK Building was, but he certainly knew how to surf the internet and use MS Word and Excel, and the hours would work out well with his classes.

"I worked as a tour guide in Alaska," answered Justin, "and used the computer system on the tours and to file reports. I also worked in an office as part of a humanitarian project in Mexico."

"Okay," said the older gentleman. He asked Justin a few basic questions about his experience and then said, "If you can agree to start today, and if you pass our basic computer literacy test, you can have the position. It's minimum campus wage, which is about a dollar an hour higher than the national minimum wage."

"Where do I take the literacy test?" Justin inquired.

"Jon can get you started and take down your information," the man responded. "By the way, I'm Kevin Markus."

"I'm Justin Murray."

Mr. Markus turned to Jon and said, "Get Justin started on the basic computer literacy test, and then if he doesn't pass, post a job at Student Services so that we can get this filled—but it has got to be done ASAP. I need to go finish a project for the CS department."

"Will do," said Jon.

Mr. Markus then excused himself, and Dan piped up in a joking tone: "So, you gonna buy the book?"

Justin laughed. "Yeah, I guess I will." He wrote out a check and put the book in his backpack.

Jon got Justin started on a computer to take the test. It took about thirty minutes, and Justin passed. Some of the questions were: "How do you open a new tab in an internet browser?" and "How do you set text in a boldface font?"

Jon took Justin's personal information for the job and commented that he had been lucky to be in the right place at the right time. Jon then gave Justin the room number for the computer lab in the MK Building.

"Just be there ten minutes before two o'clock, and I'll show you the ropes on helping people," Jon said.

"Do I need to walk up and down the aisles and find people need help?" Justin asked, trying to clarify his duties.

"No," Jon replied, "just sit at the desk and wait for someone to ask for your help."

"What do I do when no one comes to ask for help?" Justin asked.

"Some of our lab monitors read, others surf the web, others do homework or whatever—as long as you obey lab rules," Jon remarked.

Justin remembered the information desk attendant in the library earlier that day who had been reading when Justin walked by. He then realized just how good a job he had gotten: He would be getting paid to do his homework.

By then it was 10:30. Justin found out which building school financial counselors were in and went there. There was a long line of other students. The setting reminded Justin of the DMV, where hoards of people waited until a clerk was ready. There was a sign above a desk that read: "Hate to wait? Sign up for an appointment."

After waiting for several other students to use the computer on the desk, Justin made an appointment; the only time that was available was

Friday at 11 a.m. Justin decided to schedule a time to meet with a counselor instead of waiting. By Friday, he hoped to have met with someone at his bank to explore options.

School Counselors

Justin had a quick PB&J sandwich from his backpack and headed to his appointment with the counselor. He was assigned a counselor named Ms. Crawford. He told her he needed to make sure he had enough classes to be enrolled full-time.

Ms. Crawford asked for his information and pulled up his profile. "It looks like you need to have two more credit hours to be a full-time student. What classes do you want to take?"

"Do you have any classes like racquetball or tennis?" Justin asked, remembering Dave's advice to get fun classes.

"Hmm, the physical education classes are only one credit hour, so you will need to take two of them," Ms. Crawford said.

"Okay. So, are any available?" Justin asked hopefully.

"There are two openings, one at 3 p.m. and one at 5 p.m.," Ms. Crawford replied.

Since he was working from 2:30 to 6:30, Justin had to turn those down. "I have to work then. What else do you have?"

"Ballet and floor gymnastics are available."

Justin frowned as Ms. Crawford continued speaking.

"Most of the entry-level classes are full and based on your student standing and work schedule you don't have many options. But there are two 7 a.m. classes that could work. One is woodcarving, and the other is a class that opened up just today, a personal finance class."

She told Justin that students would learn to make figures from blocks of wood in the woodcarving class. The finance class was a specialty class that was being taught by a visiting professor.

Woodcarving sounded like a lot of fun, Justin thought. He had always wanted to learn how to make things with wood. He imagined himself carving birds and fish for his family and maybe for a girlfriend later. He decided to take it.

"I'll take the…" Justin began, but just then the words his grandfather had spoken to him came into his mind:

You're at an important time in your life, Justin. Learn all you can about money and how it works. The habits you establish now will stay with you for the rest of your life.

"Yes?" said Ms. Crawford, trying to evoke a response.

"I'll take the finance class," Justin said hesitantly and with a hint of longing in his voice for the "fun" class.

"Okay," Ms. Crawford said as she registered Justin as she registered him. "Huh, what's this?" she muttered as she read a pop-up window. "It appears there's a special stipulation. The professor requires each student to get his final approval before they can join the class. You need him to sign your add/drop card. There are only a few slots left, so if you will agree to get the professor's signature, I can sign you up for it."

"Okay, I can do that," Justin said.

Since classes were starting tomorrow, Justin was determined to get that signature. The class fit Justin's schedule and, luckily enough, fulfilled a beginning level math requirement; he was *going* to take the class. But first, work.

Justin went to the MK Building and met Jon, who showed him where to sit and how to log into the time-keeping system. He pointed out a poster that had the lab rules listed for all to see.

"Your job is to offer help to students who ask," said Jon. "About once every one or two hours, push the chairs in under the computer tables to help keep the lab orderly."

Justin was also given the lab door code and told that there were several codes that opened the labs.

"Don't give the code to anyone," Jon told him. "This code is tied directly to you, so if it ever gets out, you're responsible financially for anything missing or damaged."

Jon showed Justin a few more things and then left to get back to the Student I.T. room to handle things there.

The MK Building was not in the central part of campus, but there were still many students who needed to use its lab. A few asked Justin for help getting on the internet. He wondered how they had missed acquiring such a simple skill.

He wasn't allowed to talk on his cell phone during work, so he logged into his email and checked it. He then tried to study a map of the campus so he could find his classes later. By the third long, boring hour of his shift, he remembered the attendant who had been reading at the information desk in the library and wished he had brought an interesting book—good thing he would have homework to occupy him in the future.

Justin logged into his bank account and started a chat session to ask about getting a student loan. He was told that he would have to make an appointment for an in-person or telephone meeting. All of the appointment times were taken for the next two days. Justin thanked the rep and ended the chat.

School was starting tomorrow, with his first class at 7 a.m. *Why did I take a 7 a.m. class and why one that has math? Maybe I should have gone with woodworking. How am I going to pay for school? Why is this so difficult?*

The rest of the afternoon was uneventful. At the end of his shift, Justin met his replacement for the next shift, a girl named Erin. They spoke for a bit.

"Yeah, I've had this job for three semesters," Erin said. "It's kind of nice to get paid to do my homework, and believe me, my major has a lot of homework."

After leaving work, Justin remembered Paul had invited him to a movie at his place, and Justin wanted to go see it—especially since he had missed the dance. He went back to his car and found a pink "Parking Violation" notice under his windshield wiper. *Snap! I didn't realize I parked in administrative parking. I bet they hide the signs on purpose,* Justin thought, more than a little annoyed. The ticket stated, as a reminder, that parking passes could be purchased at the Campus Parking Center.

When he got to the apartment, he saw Paul with a girl that he guessed was Anna, along with several other people.

"Dude!" said Paul. "Glad you could come."

"So am I," said Justin.

"Grab some snacks," Paul said, pointing to a table containing some chips, salsa, cakes, and other goodies.

Chapter 2: Principles and Suggestions

Note: Even though the chapter mentions getting a student loan, this is something you can avoid by applying many of the strategies in this book. As the book progresses, you will note that the characters shy away from student loans.

1. Your Student ID is a valuable way to get discounts.

2. Buying books online is generally 30% to 90% cheaper. (Note to bookstores: I know ways to drastically increase profits and help you be more competitive.)
   a. Check the description. Avoid international editions.
   b. Check the time frame for shipping. Know your deadlines.

3. Jobs that Pay Big—don't overlook a job to pay for school: There are lots of jobs that don't require you to do much besides just being there. These jobs are valuable because, if you are allowed to do other things while at work, you can do your homework there. Think of this as a scholarship to do homework.

4. Take classes that teach you about personal finance early in your college program. These classes will help you understand how money works and can help to avoid debt.

Chapter 2: Assignments

Get the free workbook at *www.FindingCollegeCash.com/FreeWB*

1. Complete the exercise "Make Your Own Plan" in the workbook.

2. Investigate getting a job on campus. Even if you don't get a job, knowing your options can help you.

    a.   Use the exercise in the workbook entitled "Campus Jobs"

3. Set up an appointment to meet with a school counselor and ask about financial aid options. Don't let them convince you that the only option is to get a student loan. There are other options.

Chapter 2: Warnings and What to Avoid

1. Avoid paying too much for books. Research, ask the professor, buy online, rent, etc.

2. Don't assume that you can do homework at work. You need to check with your employer.

3. It is not necessary to get a student loan. You can avoid having a student loan altogether if you will follow many of the principles in this book.

Chapter 3
What You Should Do First

Justin's alarm rang at 6:15 a.m. *Ugh, why did I stay up past 11:30? Maybe a 7 a.m. class isn't such a good idea.* Justin got dressed, read some scripture verses, and went downstairs.

"Heard you come in last night," Dave said to Justin. "Would you mind coming in before 10:15 so that you don't wake us up when you get in?"

"Sorry," Justin said a little sheepishly. "I'll do better."

"So, did you get any *fun* classes?" Dave asked curiously.

"They were mostly all taken," Justin said.

"Mostly?" Dave asked skeptically. "What do you mean *mostly*?"

"Well, I had a choice between this financial math class and woodworking," Justin said.

"You traded woodworking for a math class?" Dave said with surprise. "I'm telling you, man, the fun classes are the ones that you need to be takin'. You'll thank me later."

Not knowing how to respond to his cousin's remarks, Justin just agreed and said "'Kay, thanks" as he left.

Justin hoped that he could quickly ask the professor to sign his add/drop card if he arrived early. He found the class and sat in the second row. There were about thirty other students in the room. The teacher was at his desk, not looking at anyone, finishing something on the computer. The bell rang, and the professor rose from his desk.

Very sternly the professor announced, "Class, I am Professor Christensen, and I *will* be addressed as such."

"In this class, I am going to teach you principles that—if you follow them—will help you earn money and manage money so you can avoid student loans and common financial traps college students fall into."

The professor started a PowerPoint presentation with a click of the remote in his hand. A slide with the words "Today's Agenda" across the slide came up. Then the screen changed and showed a bulleted list:

- Class rules
- Syllabus
- Grading
- Lesson

Class Rules

SECTION NOTE: Pay attention to the class rules presented below as these same rules can help you in writing essays and applying for financial resources.

"Rule number one," Professor Christensen announced as the slide changed. "*Nothing* late will be accepted."

As he was speaking, two more students filed in. "Ah, just in time," said Professor Christensen snidely. "We are discussing class rules, and we are on the topic of being late."

"Okay, whatever," said one of the students who was late.

"We haven't gotten there yet, but you all will still need a signature from me to add this class and without it, you will *not* be taking this class. The world is full of people who think that they are entitled to special privileges. Let me be clear, this class is not going to be an easy class. You won't be able to just show up and get an 'A.' As it is in life, so it will be in this class: Any privileges you enjoy are either given to you by others or earned. However, this will be a rewarding class.

"Some of you will come here and just try to squeak by," Professor Christensen continued. "That isn't going to work in this class, and why rule number one is so important. Some of you will work for an employer, and hopefully you will *not* one day say to your boss, 'Gee, boss, I know that I didn't get the report in on time and that as a result we lost the prestigious Johnson account we were going to get, but here's the report, done the way you asked, even though it's late—at least I hope it's done the way you wanted. Maybe you can go to Mr. Johnson and ask him if we can have partial credit for trying to get things done the way we promised we would.'

"If any of you ever have that conversation with your boss, I hope that you've kept your résumé polished because your job will be very much in jeopardy. Life doesn't usually allow make-ups or partial credit. *If you are not ready to catch opportunity when it comes, the opportunity will not wait for you,*" Professor Christensen said with emphasis.

"Don't you mean that no late *work* will be accepted, instead of *nothing* late will be accepted?" asked a guy behind Justin.

"No, I mean *nothing* late will be accepted. This includes anyone who comes late to class. You see, most days we will be going on a field trip, and we will leave right at 7 a.m. If you are not here, then you are not coming. Additionally, I will be locking the door at 7. If you are not in the room, you will miss the discussion and the assignments. And if you think you can just ask your classmates which assignments are the ones needed for any particular day, believe me: I will check your attendance. All assignments are due by the deadline specified on the class website."

Professor Christensen clicked the remote to advance the slides. The following rules appeared one by one:

Rule #1: Nothing late will be accepted. No exceptions.

Rule #2: All submissions must be spellchecked, free of errors, written using good grammar, and in compliance with submission requirements.

Rule #3: Respect other people and their beliefs.

Rule #4: All submitted work is final. No redo chances!

Rule #5: Participation is mandatory and will affect your grade.

Rule #6: Act with integrity in everything; do not allow anyone to do any-thing that violates personal integrity or class rules.

Rule #7: Seek and give help. If you need help, ask for help. If someone asks for help, help as you are able.

Rule #8: Express gratitude for all help received.

Rule #9: Maintain a positive attitude.

Rule #10: Take good care of your body, mind, and spirit. [9]

"Any questions?" Professor Christensen asked the class.

"What if we have a school-excused absence or are sick? Shouldn't we be allowed to make up work?" asked a girl to the right of Justin.

"If you're going to be absent on a class day," answered the professor, "you will need to finish and submit the assignments before then. Most ath-letes know when games, practices, and out-of-school events are going to be held. You will need to notify me before the fact. As for being sick, you had better get a doctor's note and be bedridden. Remember the rule: We take good care of our bodies, minds, and spirits."

"What constitutes acting with integrity? How are you going to know whether or not we acted with integrity?" asked a guy to Justin's left.

The professor's gaze settled on him firmly when he responded: "There are certain principles and laws in this universe. Sir Isaac Newton said, 'For every action, there is an equal and opposite reaction.'[10] This principle applies in physics and in everyday life. You cannot acquire true wealth by being dishonest. This means that if you try to cheat in other classes, lie to

---

9   These same rules will help as you apply for scholarships and other resources for col-lege. For example, be on time with submissions, be respectful, use a positive written tone, etc.

10 The Physics Classroom. "Newton's Third Law." Accessed August 9, 2017. http://www.physicsclassroom.com/class/newtlaws/Lesson-4/Newton-s-Third-Law.

someone, or act with dishonesty, you'll soon find that others will not trust you, your relationships will suffer, and you will lower your own self-esteem and lower your feelings of self-worth.

"*You must act with honor to receive honorable gains*; anything else destroys happiness and lessens your wealth, cheapens you, and burdens you with guilt. True, many people cheat and lie to get money fraudulently, but those people do not have true wealth, demean themselves, sabotage their relationships, and diminish their future opportunities.

"We should only do those things that leave everyone better off than how we found them and enhance humanity in the process. I will be teaching you how to acquire wealth by applying principles. While you may get money by being dishonest, *true wealth comes from increasing your quality of life in every area of your life*—and your character is part of your wealth.

"If we treat others harshly, others will oppose us harshly. When we are honest in all areas of our lives and act with integrity, we are trusted by others and can have self-respect and dignity.

"In this class, each of us has the right to express our beliefs and that shouldn't offend anyone. If someone tells you 'good luck!' it shouldn't offend you that someone wishes you well—even if you don't believe in luck. Consider any reference anyone else makes to their personal beliefs in the same way. We can learn from others' beliefs that are different from our own, even if we don't agree on every point.[11] I don't believe Aesop's fables literally, but I still value the lessons they teach me, and I am not offended when I hear "The Tortoise and the Hare" even though I doubt that such a race ever occurred. In this class, we'll respect the beliefs of every individual in the class. I will use anything from poetry to ancient texts if I feel that it will help teach a financial concept."

---

11 As you submit essays and apply for scholarships, please share your beliefs and views in a way that is respectful. On this same note, you may disagree with other people's beliefs, but you can share your beliefs in a way that doesn't attack the beliefs of others.

Professor Christensen continued, "Next is the syllabus portion of today's class," he said, advancing the slide.

- Housing
- Business
- Scholarships and Grants
- Money Smarts

- Banking
- Online Models
- Investing
- Money Seeds

"Don't worry too much about these points right now; we'll cover all of them," said Professor Christensen. "Let me show you how grading works."

- Assignments: 35%
- Class Participation: 10%
- Teacher Evaluation: 55%. Ongoing and completely subjective assessments will be made throughout the semester and at the end of the term.

"What!" cried several students.

"What do you mean, it's subjective and ongoing?" one of the class members dared to ask.

"It means," responded Professor Christensen, "that, per your question earlier about integrity, if I learn that you were dishonest in any area of your life—that you cheated, lied, acted disrespectfully about another's beliefs, broke another rule, and/or chose to intentionally neglect an assignment, I have the right to reduce 55% of your grade as low as I desire. I get to decide how you fare, completely subjectively, based on my evaluations. You can try to scrape by, but all it will take is one dishonest event and your grade will drop. This is my class, and these are my rules. If anyone here doesn't want to abide by these rules and this grading system, there is the door." Professor Christensen pointed at the classroom door.

With those words, the same student packed up his belongings and huffed out the door, mumbling, "I'm not leaving my grade up to a whimsical tyrant who won't even give me a fair grading scale."

Professor Christensen smiled. "I love it when they do that," he said wryly. "Anyone else? You might as well leave now because this course is not going to get any easier," he said with an expectant look on his face.

Two more students got up and left. Professor Christensen's smile widened. It was the kind of smile that made Justin wonder if he enjoyed watching students suffer. Justin thought about the woodworking class again. *Maybe this was a bad idea, taking this class.* His thoughts were interrupted by Professor Christensen.

"Do you think those students were victors or victims? Do you think they were people who chose to *act* or to be acted *upon* by life and circumstances? Do you think they blamed me and the class or were willing to take responsibility for their own thoughts, emotions, and actions?"

"Victims," replied a girl in the back of the class. Justin turned to look at her and saw that she was *really* cute.

"Attitude is always a choice," the girl added.

"Very good," said Professor Christensen. "Victor Frankl said, 'The one thing you can't take away from me is the way I choose to respond to what you do to me. The last of one's freedoms is to choose one's attitude in any given circumstance.'[12] Sadly, most people choose to give this freedom away first; they let other people and circumstances control how they respond, rather than choosing for themselves. As Ms.—" Professor Christensen paused, trying to evoke a name, gesturing toward the girl who had spoken.

"Pratt, Allison Pratt," the girl responded.

"As Ms. Pratt said, attitude is a choice." The mood in the room changed from self-pity to wonder. "We will come back to this point later, but this brings us to rule number 11," Professor Christensen said as he changed the PowerPoint slide. "We take full responsibility for our thoughts, emotions, actions, and results," he read aloud.

---

12 Google Books. "Man's Search for Meaning - Viktor Emil Frankl." Accessed April 19, 2017. http://books.google.com/books?id=F-Q_xGjWBi8C.

Introduction to College Costs

"Now, enough jibber-jabber," Professor Christensen said. "Let's get on to today's lesson." He changed the slide: "Housing and Properties."

"We are going to begin at the beginning. Many students when they go to college end up spending too much money for an apartment. They also fail to understand the full cost of college after accounting for food, utilities, fun money—in addition to college costs like tuition and class fees. We are going to address these right now.

"All unmarried students, tell me honestly, how much does it cost to rent a room here? Just shout out your monthly rent."

Justin's ears perked; he still needed to find a place to live. The students began shouting out their answers:

"$295 shared room."

"$285, shared."

"$490, private."

$450, private room."

"$255, shared."

"Free, I live at home."

$310 for a shared room."

After about a half-dozen other responses, Professor Christensen interrupted, "All right, the average is about $300 a month for a shared room and $475 for a private room. We are going to ignore the summer terms, and just assume that you go to school year-round. If you want to break down the costs, you can look on the SSU website for a cost breakdown."

Bringing up a spreadsheet on the overhead screen, Professor Christensen typed in:

$300 per month x 12 months per year x 4 years = $14,400
$475 per month x 12 months per year x 4 years = $22,800

"Now, how much do you spend on food each month, or your meal plan for a month?" Professor Christensen asked.

Answers rang out. The amount averaged about $275 per month. Professor Christensen entered:

$275 per month x 12 months per year x 4 years = $13,200

"How much do you spend on books each semester?" Professor Christensen asked intently.

As students gave their responses, Justin was amazed. *Holy cow! Paul was right. People are spending $600 to $1,200 on books. I am so grateful Paul took the time to teach me how to get them for less.*

Professor Christensen added the average amount to the spreadsheet: $800 per semester x 8 semesters = $6,400

After typing in tuition for eight semesters, Professor Christensen said: "You are lucky to be attending Syracuse State University; some schools charge more than $30,000 a year for tuition," he said. "However, even here, you can easily see why students end up in debt when they go to college."

Justin felt really uneasy. He knew that college was going to be expensive, and he knew the tuition rates, but he had never taken the time to add up his total costs. *How am I ever going to pay for college?* Justin thought. *I mean, this is expensive.* Justin started to feel that he needed to work on getting a student loan fast.

As if Professor Christensen could read Justin's thoughts, he said, "Some of you are asking yourselves 'How am I going to pay for college?' and then you immediately and ignorantly start thinking that you are going to rush down—if you haven't already—to your bank or student loan officer to take out the total amount we calculated in one lump sum."

Professor Christensen's tone changed from stoic to irritated and intense. "Why would you pay for your senior year at the beginning of your freshman year and then accumulate interest for four years?"

Some members of the class had looks of contemplation on their faces. Without waiting for an answer, Professor Christensen continued.

"Yes, some of the federal student loans are subsidized during the time that you are enrolled at least half-time, but that doesn't mean there is no interest. The government pays the interest, but who provides the money to the government? The taxpayers. And then to make matters worse, you are enslaving yourself to about two decades of debt after college. Why are you even going to college if you're are going to spend the equivalent of a second mortgage each month paying a student loan for a decade or two, netting about the same income you would have had without college? Worse, a student loan is one of the few legal loans that's non-forgivable—meaning that even if you declared bankruptcy, the debt would still be yours to pay. As a taxpayer myself, I'd rather give you the money than put you into that kind of a mess.

"You probably never thought about it before," Professor Christensen continued, his tone softening, "but it is important you understand what it really means to get a student loan."

Assignment Set 1

"I would like to help everyone here pay for college, manage your finances, and grow your personal wealth," Professor Christensen said in a more cheerful tone.

"First, I want you to find at least ten different ads for housing. I also want you to look at the dorms and see what it costs to live on-campus. You will need to scan these ads to the class website." Professor Christensen said. "Please indicate for each ad whether the cost includes utilities or they are separately billed."

There were groans from several students and murmured complaints. "It's too late now that the semester has begun." "Why are we being asked to do this now?"

"You will need my signature on an add/drop card," Professor Christensen went on in a tone of authority.

A spikey-haired guy raised his hand and said defiantly, "Look, I'm already under contract to rent a very expensive apartment. There is no way that I'm going to waste my time looking for another place to live when I can't change where I live even if I wanted to." Several other students nodded in agreement.

"That's fine," said Professor Christensen. "I really could care less if you actually change your place of residence. However, like any other class, this class comes with assignments, and if you want to be in this class, you need to do this assignment before Saturday at 8 p.m. If you haven't done this assignment by then, don't bother showing up Monday morning. I'm not teaching a class on how to make excuses. I'm teaching a class on building wealth. Go cry to your girlfriend, tell a sob story to your parents, and report me to the department head and dean of the university. Not one of them will get me to change my mind on this topic, and not one of them can ensure you a seat in my class. I just want you to be aware of the options available to you. For your information, it is possible, in some cases, to sell your contract to another student or cancel your lease—if it is still within the first few days. You could even pay the separation fee if you were to save enough money. There are always choices. I'm trying to help you understand the choices you do have."

"Do you have any idea who I am?" asked the spikey-haired guy.

"Yes," said Professor Christensen, "you are a temporary student in my class."

"My father is Dan Fredrickson, head partner at Fredrickson, Beecher, and Grant, city councilman, and member of the board of directors of the university," the guy said arrogantly.

"That's not who you are," said the Professor. "A moment ago you asked me if I knew who *you* are, not who your father is. Everything you just told me is about you riding on your father's good name and your father's hard work. You didn't even state your name. Do you expect to coast through life riding on the coattails, good name, and fortune of your father? If that's your hope, you need to leave my class."

"First, it's Malcolm, and second I can't leave!" replied the spiky-haired guy curtly. "My father, for some strange reason, said that I have to take this class—but I don't have to like it."

"Oh, *poor baby*," said the professor sarcastically.

There was obvious tension in the room, and Justin was feeling uncomfortable. He took a breath, raised his hand, and said, "Excuse me, Professor. With no disrespect, aren't you breaking your own rule about keeping a positive attitude and possibly the one about another's beliefs by going off on Malcolm?"

Silence. Then something happened that made Justin believe that maybe he had just made the worse decision ever. Professor Christensen's face held a hint of a smile, as though he were trying to stifle laughter. Justin couldn't tell if the professor was relishing the moment or trying *not* to enjoy the students' suffering. The professor looked coldly at Justin.

"What is your name?" the professor asked Justin, who was trying to maintain his composure.

"Justin Murray." He spoke up with as much confidence as he could muster.

"You are on dangerous ground, Mr. Murray," Professor Christensen said. "Nevertheless, thank you for helping us to transition to the next assignment." The professor advanced the slides on the PowerPoint. The tension was gone, just like that. "For this next assignment, you will begin to look for financing sources. You will begin by using a well-known website. Let's take a look."

Assignment Set 2

1. Go to www.fafsa.ed.gov/.
   a. Fill out a Free Application for Federal Student Aid, or FAFSA.
   b. Do a screen capture of the completed submission number—you may mask any personal information, including your email address.

"Submit the profile on the class website by 8:00 p.m. on Saturday," the professor said. "This assignment must be completed before subsequent assignments. Many of the websites we will use in future assignments require a completed FAFSA before a submission is attempted."

There were several whispered gripes about "not knowing how to do this," it being "only for poor people," and "being a time-waster."

"With the exception of Mr. Fredrickson, whose father apparently has some leverage with him, no one is making you take this class," Professor Christensen commented.

Malcolm glared in disgust.

"However," the professor continued, "what I am going to do is cancel Friday's class so that you can have time to accomplish all that I ask of you. You need to have all the assignment sets done and submitted by Saturday at 8:00 p.m. and then, if you have those done, you can come Monday and I will sign your add/drop card so you can be formally admitted to the class."

"Wait—isn't Monday the add/drop deadline for classes?" a girl behind Justin asked.

"My, you are perceptive," said Professor Christensen. "You can see the assignments and then decide if you want to complete them or you can leave now. Either way, it is your choice." He made no further reply but advanced the next slide.

Assignment Set 3

"For the following two assignments," Professor Christensen continued, "the Campus Student Writing Center may be helpful for any reports, essays, or submissions. Get a writing TA to review your work."

Choose **ONE** of the following:

1. Go to fastweb.com or bigfuture.collegeboard.org/scholarship-search; fill out a profile.

    a.   Search for scholarships.

    b.   Click the links to several different scholarships.

    c.   Read the scholarship requirements.

    d.   Apply for **TWO** different scholarships.

    e.   Save a copy of what you submitted (i.e. essays, photos, etc.) and the scholarship requirements in separate files in a folder on your computer, portable hard drive, or web drive.

2. Go to the Campus Scholarship Department and/or the department for your major.

    a.   Schedule an appointment with a counselor.

    b.   Ask about scholarships that may be available to you based on your student profile.

        i.   Follow the instructions given to you by your counselor.

        ii.   Often, you will submit the application Online.

        iii.   Either provide confirmation of the submission, or, if you apply by mail, provide copies of the scholarship requirements and items you submitted (e.g., essay).

    c.   Fill out a profile as listed above in (1) at fastweb.com or bigfuture.collegeboard.org/scholarship-search.

        i.   Submit **ONE** scholarship application, following the steps listed under (1), and submit a screenshot.

Professor Christensen announced to the class, "Please take note that you will only be able to make submissions until Saturday night at 8 p.m. After that, if you have not submitted all assignments, you will not be in the class."

"Professor—" Allison said tentatively while raising her hand.

"Yes," said Professor Christensen.

"Professor," Allison continued, "why are you telling us to apply for two scholarships without even showing us how? Would you please teach us what to do and how to do this so we can avoid wasting our time?"

"Aw," said Professor Christensen with a tone of amusement, "I assume you think that applying for scholarships and financial aid is a waste of time—probably because you feel that you won't get it, so why bother? Am I correct?"

"Well, I—" Allison began. Justin could tell that she was choosing her words carefully. "I understand that these are the assignments and that if I would like to remain in the class I need to complete them—as I would for any other class. But beyond just fulfilling the requirements, I would like to know what I am doing so that I might actually have a chance of being considered by the scholarship judges, to avoid wasting my time or just doing busywork. I am asking because one of your rules said that if we ask for help, we receive help or something like that. I want more than just to do the assignment, I want to know how to do it correctly, so I can actually have a chance at the money offered."

"Very well stated, Ms. Pratt," Professor Christensen said in a stoic, but questioning tone. "Does anyone else hold similar beliefs?"

Several students nodded in agreement, but no one voiced an opinion. Justin felt hesitant because he wanted to see what would happen next.

Professor Christensen spoke deliberately, with earnestness, "Ms. Pratt, I commend you for seeing beyond the assignment. Let me share with you three things that could greatly help you in your assessment of this class. First, this will be a weekly assignment; each week, all class members will be required to apply for two scholarships."

There were several moans.

Without stopping to comment, Professor Christensen doggedly continued: "Second, yes, we will be discussing more about how to apply for scholarships and other resources throughout the semester. Third, precisely why I am having you apply to scholarships now is that the biggest chance of success is often created by just showing up. I realize you won't be perfect at it, and I know that it seems like a waste of time. I anticipate the frustration you will feel. Yet, I am helping you to get started; you don't have the time to waste worrying about technique and procedure. Just get the assignments done. Stop worrying about perfection; it is more important that you get the scholarship submissions turned in than it is to wait to do them perfectly and perhaps miss the opportunity to apply."

Allison sheepishly said "Thanks," but did not say more. Justin wondered if she felt she had been silenced.

Professor Christensen changed the PowerPoint slide. It read:

Assignment Set 4

For this following assignment set, make a plan for how to accomplish the tasks. This assignment is to prepare for other tasks. Do all of the following:

1. Pick a charity to give 10% of your income to; even if your income is zero, pick a charity you would *like* to give 10% to.

2. Decide upon activities that you can do to give at least one hour of service every week. This can include tutoring, yard work, babysitting, religious service, cleaning, assisting a professor, or humanitarian service. If needed, use the free JustServe app from the Apple, Google Play, or Windows app store. More instructions will come later.

3. Decide upon some uplifting books—no textbooks—that you will read every morning for fifteen minutes. You may choose self-help books, religious books, or other positive uplifting literature.

Create a plan for completing the previous assignments. Submit your plan on the class website by Saturday at 8 p.m.

"There is no class on Friday this week," Professor Christensen announced. "Remember to do these four assignment sets. Those of you who do these assignments by Saturday at 8 p.m. and who arrive Monday before 7 a.m. will be added to the class on Monday.

"You're going to have to take a chance," he continued in a cold tone. "If you want to be in this class, you need to decide. I am not going to make it easy for you.

It's going to be a grueling semester, and you may wonder why you ever decided to take this class. Yet, if you do what I've outlined, it will be very rewarding, as I can teach you how to implement the principles of building wealth. You know the class rules. You have seen how I interact with others. You should know that I have NO tolerance for nonsense or for work that is less than your best."

There was a somber silence in the room. The bell rang; it was now 8:50—the end of a two-hour block.

Justin started to pack up his things. The professor said, "Mr. Murray, I need to speak with you before you go."

A guy passing Justin spoke into his ear. "If he tries to get you to do a "Heil Hitler," remind him this is America and we have something here called courtesy."

Under his breath, Justin answered sarcastically, "Thanks."

Chapter 3: Principles and Suggestions

1. The number one reason people don't get scholarships and grants is that they do not apply. Apply early; apply often.

2. The class rules in this chapter are actually ideas to help win scholarships.

3. Start to think in new ways. Just because you're a student doesn't mean you need to do things the same way everyone else does.

4. Be willing to stand up for your beliefs. No one has the right to criticize your worth or undermine your integrity.

5. Consider where you are headed to college. A more expensive school does *not* guarantee a higher-paying job.

Chapter 3: Assignments

Get the free workbook at *www.FindingCollegeCash.com/FreeWB*

1. Visit your campus writing center. Having someone like a teacher or tutor look over your essays before you submit them will be extremely helpful.

2. Complete the "Housing Questions" exercise in the workbook.

3. Go to *www.fafsa.gov*. Fill out a profile.

4. Do either of the following:
   a. Fill out a profile at either fastweb.com or bigfuture.collegeboard.org/scholarship-search; or
   b. Go to your department office, ask about scholarships, and then fill out a profile for one of them at one of the resources in (a).

5. Make a plan to
   a. Give away 10% of your income to a charitable cause;
   b. Give at least one hour of unpaid service per week (use the free JustServe app to find opportunities to serve); and
   c. Find a positive book that you can read each day for fifteen minutes. Consider self-help, religious, and other uplifting books.

Chapter 3: Warnings and What to Avoid

1. Do your best to keep your GPA up to increase your chances of being awarded a scholarship. However, GPA does not always determine eligibility.

2. It is better for you to turn in an imperfect application and essay than it is to try to create a perfect application and never apply. Go ahead and get started. You will learn more as you continue to read the book.

Chapter 4
The Proof is in the Pudding

Justin couldn't imagine why Professor Christensen wanted to speak with him, but he made his way to the front of the room.

"Mr. Murray," Professor Christensen said, stern as ever, and looking Justin in the eye, "that was a very brave thing that you did earlier—standing up for someone whom you may not even know."

"Well, I—" Justin started, but he was cut off.

"I am going to give you some information that may be of use to you. First, I would like you to take this class. I admire people who can stand up for others and hold fast to their principles. Second, things are not always what they seem; in order to find gold, you often have to search for it in places where other people are afraid to venture or may not think to look. You may go now, Mr. Murray," the professor dismissed him abruptly as he gestured toward the door.

Justin walked away confused. *What was that all about?* Justin wondered as he made his way to his next class. *Why did he want to talk to me? Why did he compliment me and tell me he wants me to take this class but then seem so rude and abrupt and like a jerk? Is he going to pick fights with me all semester? I mean, what's this guy's problem? We're just students, and he was coming down on nearly everyone who offered an opinion. I still need to pay for school. Why am I taking this class anyway?*

Justin's next class passed with much less drama. In fact, it was kind of boring; most of the class time was spent going over the syllabus and grading policies. His mind wandered back to his finance class that morning. *Well,* he thought, *if the class turns out to be a disaster, at least there's that cute girl…*

Justin's third class passed about the same way as the second—no drama and a lot of logistical information. Since he had a thirty-minute break before his next class, he decided that he would call his bank to see about getting a student loan.

Some Downsides to Student Loans

"I need to read you some disclosures," a loan officer at Justin's bank said. "You will not be able to rid yourself of the loan. Even if you declare bankruptcy, you will still be responsible for the loan amount. Because this is an unsubsidized loan, interest will accrue during the time that you are in school. At any point that you stop going to school, you will start the payment clock—you will be required to start making payments to pay back the loan with interest accumulated. Having a student loan may hinder you from getting additional loans, such as a mortgage. This is a serious financial obligation that may permanently affect you. Do you wish to continue with the loan?"

Justin gave his information, stating that he would be attending school full-time. The representative gave him the loan rate and payback schedule if all went as planned. "Would you like to borrow money to pay for things like rent and living costs?"

Wait! Justin thought, *Paul said to at least compare options. Before I sign my life away, I should keep my appointment with the school financial counselor.* "I'm meeting with a financial counselor from the school on Friday. Now that I know what you're offering, may I come into a branch if your offer is better?"

"That will be fine," the rep said. They ended the call.

At least I can check to see who offers me a better deal, Justin thought as he hung up the phone. *Will never go away? Interest accrues while in school—so the balance keeps going up?! May hinder my financial future?! What kind of service is that? That seems more like slavery. I had better be careful before I sign up for a student loan. I'm glad Paul told me to compare several offers.*

Justin went to the rest of his classes and was finally finished with school by 1:50 p.m. At work, several students needed Justin's help to try to get their student computer accounts set up. One asked, "What are those little red squiggles under the words in my essay in MS Word?" Justin had to hold back his laughter.

Applying with FAFSA

During a lull at work, Justin started working on an essay, but then he remembered that he had to go to *www.fafsa.ed.gov* and complete his FAFSA. He went to the website and filled out the form. He knew how to answer most of the questions, but there were several he needed to ask his mom. He emailed her and then logged into a social media account for a break.

Pling! went Justin's chat window. There was a message from Paul. "Dude, what's up? How were classes today?"

"Fine—kind of boring, most of them," Justin typed.

"Most?" Paul asked.

"Well, in my first class, the professor seemed to be a real jerk," Justin replied.

"Ditch the class, if you can, and move on," Paul advised. "Any cute girls?☺"

"In the same class with the professor who was a jerk, there was a really cute girl."

"What's her name?"

"Allison Pratt."

"Did you get her number?"

"No," typed Justin. "I only found out her name because the teacher was grilling several students."

"That's OK," Paul wrote.

"Excuse me," said a student in the computer lab. Justin turned and saw a guy standing there.

"Got to go," Justin typed. "Work is calling." He closed the chat session and helped the student with some formatting for a paper.

Returning to his desk, he found another chat message was open. It was his mom.

"Hi, sweetie. How were classes?"

Not wanting to worry her, Justin wrote, "Okay. It was mostly just going over the syllabi. Mom, did you get my email?"

"I haven't checked my email yet. What was it about?" she asked.

"A teacher is having us fill out the FAFSA form for an assignment."

"I've heard about those, but didn't know how to get one," said Justin's mother. "It's good that you're filling it out, especially with Dad's income being what it is."

"Yeah, I guess so. I need to know if I'm going to be claimed as a dependent for tax purposes and what Dad's income for last year was," Justin typed.

"On last year's taxes, we filed your taxes as an independent. I'll look at our last return to get the income amounts."

"Thanks, Mom," Justin said.

"Have you found a place to stay?" his mom asked, obviously implying a place *not* with Dave and Susan.

"Not yet," Justin said. "There's a website where people post rooms available, and there's also a student board where ads are posted."

"Well, don't wait too long," his mom said.

"Yeah, I know. Actually, the same teacher who gave the assignment about the FAFSA gave another assignment to go to Student Housing, and I found out that the university requires students to live in places that are approved for student housing."

"It sounds like this teacher is teaching you a lot," his mom replied.

"I guess so," Justin said.

"I'll check on Dad's income and answer your email later today," his mom promised.

"Thanks, Mom."

"Sure thing, I love you. Dad and I are praying for you."

"Thanks, Mom, love you too."

The chat session ended.

Justin decided to write that essay and start his reading assignments. After writing a few paragraphs, he got up to straighten up the lab. Later, after his paper was finished, his brain felt like mush. He checked his email. *No message from Mom yet. At least I can go and fill out a profile at that Fastweb place. I don't have my FAFSA done, but maybe I can get around that.*

Scholarship Starts—Seeing What Is Out There

He went to fastweb.com and completed his profile. There were questions about his parents, his religion, his hobbies, his major, where he had lived, his likes, and even some questions about his past schooling. In high school, he had had a 3.06 GPA and had gotten a score of 23 on the ACT. *Okay,* he thought to himself before clicking the final submit button, *I'll bet there are only three scholarships open to me at this point. I mean, you've basically got to have a 4.0 and 30-something on the ACT to get a scholarship.* Justin hit "submit" and the Fastweb website indicated the scholarships available to him.

"Whoa!" Justin said softly to himself. "I really don't believe this happened! Score!"

The website indicated that if he were to get all 83 scholarships available over the next year, he would have $187,418 available for his use. He clicked on the scholarship that had the soonest submission deadline. He read the scholarship description and then the requirements. It was for $2,000. Justin saw that one of the requirements was completing the FAFSA profile. *Okay, Professor Christensen, you've piqued my interest. Maybe you do know what you're talking about—we'll see,* Justin thought. He marked a few of the scholarships as his favorites, and then signed out of the site.

He did a final check of his email fifteen minutes before his shift ended and found that his mom had replied with the information he needed for his FAFSA. Justin logged back onto his FAFSA profile and quickly completed it. After hitting the "submit" button, he was shocked to see that he had been awarded a federal Pell Grant in the amount of half a semester's tuition.[13] That was money that he didn't have to work for. *Maybe I don't need the student loan after all?* Justin mused.

Justin was excited. The Pell Grant was going to be sent to the Campus Tuition Department, not to Justin directly. He made a .pdf of the submission, which showed the amount. He quickly packed up his belongings and logged off the computer. Erin would arrive soon, and it was time to go. Professor Christensen may be rigid, but he certainly knew what he was doing.

Justin went back to Dave's house to eat dinner. As he ate, he examined housing ads. He made appointments to go that night and see some places that seemed promising. After driving around and looking at several nearby places, Justin finally visited one place that he particularly liked. He arranged to move in by the end of the week. He would share a room with a guy named Nate. Justin was glad to find a place.

Reusing Scholarship Essays and Applications

The next day, while he was at work in the computer lab he found the final two ads for his housing assignment and submitted it. He also finished up an essay for another class. He logged back on to fastweb.com and looked again at the requirements for the scholarships he had liked. One of them required an essay on essentially the same topic as the essay he had just written for a class. Justin looked at the paper he had written and wondered if it was good enough to submit. He contacted the student writing lab and set up an appointment to have his essay reviewed after work so that he could submit

---

13 FAFSA really takes 3–14 business days, but for the story's sake, it was instantaneous. Plan ahead.

it as part of the scholarship application.[14] He decided that he'd at least meet with a scholarship counselor, from the department that was over his major, to see if there were any scholarships available to him. And since he didn't have class tomorrow morning, he could meet then, before he saw the financial counselor.

When Justin finished work, he went to the writing lab. A tutor reviewed Justin's essay and gave him some tips on how to cite the sources a little better and improve the grammar. Justin then edited and improved the paper, both for class and for the scholarship application. *Awesome! Killing two birds with one stone!*

At Dave and Susan's house that night, Justin used their computer to apply for the scholarship, submitting his essay. As he copied his essay from MS Word to the online form, he noticed, on Dave and Susan's desk, a bill that was stamped "Overdue." Justin didn't pry, but he realized that his cousin was not doing as well financially as he had thought.

Dave came into the room and asked how Justin was.

"Things are going all right," Justin said, trying to act normal after seeing the bill.

"Whatcha up to?" Dave asked as he came in the room.

"Just workin' on some homework," Justin said.

"I'm telling you, man, you have got to take some fun classes, or you won't be able to enjoy your college time as much," Dave said with a friendly tone.

Remembering the bill he had seen, Justin replied, "Yeah, you're probably right ... Hey—by the way, may I pay you something for the food and time spent here?" he offered.

"No, don't worry about it. Glad to help," Dave replied.

Justin wasn't so sure.

---

14 Please check with both your college and the scholarship provider to determine if you can use homework essays as part of a scholarship application.

Meeting with Scholarship Counselors in Your Major

The next morning, Justin met with a department scholarship counselor over his major. The counselor was a man in his mid-forties who wanted to be called Bob. He looked over Justin's student profile on the computer screen.

"For freshmen, we have two scholarships you can apply for," Bob said. "One is for doing some research and then writing a paper—that one is for half tuition. The other scholarship is for $500, and you have to write a paper."

"What do I have to do to apply?" Justin asked.

"You'll need to..." Bob started reading off the scholarship requirements. "Why don't I just print these off for you, instead?"

He handed the pages to Justin. "You'll need to hurry to submit those," Bob said. "The deadline for the $500 one is Monday. You can email me the completed applications."

Justin thanked Bob and put the papers away.

"Be sure to come back when you're a sophomore. There's a full-tuition scholarship that our department offers. By the way, have you tried the Campus Scholarship Department? They have a lot of scholarships that are available to students. Often, there are not as many applicants as you would think, so you should definitely apply there," Bob stated as he looked at Justin.

"Where are they located?" Justin asked.

"They're in the Student Center on the third floor. In fact, I have access to their calendars. Let me check to see when someone is available to talk to you," Bob said as he turned back to his computer. "There's a slot available in ten minutes; if you hurry, you can make it. Would you like to take it?"

"Sure," Justin replied. He figured that since this appointment had been brief, he might as well take the opportunity to find out what the Campus Scholarship Department had to offer.

At the Campus Scholarship Department, Justin was sent by the department secretary to the office of the counselor Bob had arranged for him to meet, Mr. Wheatley, who asked him some questions. After he was finished, Mr. Wheatley said, "Hey, good news! Your father's company has a scholarship fund here at the school. All incoming freshmen get a $120 scholarship to buy books."

"What if I already bought my books?" Justin asked hopefully, remembering how Paul had helped him earlier, and trying not to wonder if his dad's company could afford to keep the scholarship fund going.

"You can pocket the money if you submit your receipts," Mr. Wheatley said.

"What do I have to do?" Justin asked.

"Just tell me which branch your father works for and his full name, so they can track it down."

Justin gave him the information, and Mr. Wheatley submitted it. "Okay, it looks like this will be verified and then credited to your student account in about a week. When it arrives, you can go to the cashier's office and get a check from them. You should also apply to the general scholarship fund. The university offers full, half, and quarter scholarships from this fund. There are more scholarships available later for sophomores, juniors, and seniors. And there are some scholarships if you join an honor society or club."

"How do I apply?" Justin asked.

"You fill out an application on our website and then get a teacher recommendation," Mr. Wheatley responded. "The teacher can send the letter of recommendation to the email address listed here." He pointed to the email address on the website. "Don't worry—you can find us on the university website, searching for scholarships. However, you do need to have this done by Monday, to meet the deadline."

"Why Monday?" Justin asked.

"It's the add/drop deadline, and scholarships must be accounted for by then. Think of it as an airplane standby. If there's a seat available you may get a ride, or you might be changed to another flight, but if you don't at least submit a request with a standby ticket, you won't get to fly on the plane, even if there *is* a vacant seat. Scholarships work the same way. If there is one available, you may get it, but if you don't at least apply, then you won't get it, even if there *is* one that could work for you." Mr. Wheatley replied as if he had that example prepared in advance.

Justin thanked him and left the room, feeling a bit gleeful. He had just received $120 because of his father's work, and all he'd had to do was spend fifteen minutes with a counselor!

Justin was hungry but thought that he could wait till he was back at Dave and Susan's house. As Justin passed the food court in the Student Center, he saw Allison, the girl from his finance class, working at one of the food vendors. Justin decided to go buy some food at her station. *Money is tight, I'll skip two meals later, but at least I can talk to her,* Justin thought as he approached her counter.

"Hey, aren't you in that personal finance class?" Allison asked Justin.

"Yeah, I think so," Justin said, trying not to sound as if he had paid much attention to her in class.

"What do you think of our professor?" Allison asked.

"He seems a little rough around the edges, but I was already able to get half the cost of tuition by filling out my FAFSA, plus I got a $120 scholarship because of my dad's work."

"Good for you!" Allison said. "What did you do to get the scholarship?"

"Spent fifteen minutes with the school counselor and answered some questions. I only met with the counselor because I was trying to fulfill Professor Christensen's assignment to apply for scholarships," Justin replied.

"You got $120 for fifteen minutes, plus half your tuition covered with your FAFSA just because you were following the professor's assignment?!" Allison asked incredulously.

"Well, yes, and he did kind of help me with housing, but I just don't want to be challenged on every point with his 'my rules, my class, there's the door' attitude," Justin replied.

"Your total is $8.41," Allison said. She looked pensive.

"Ouch," said Justin. "You don't happen to have any discounts or coupons circulating?" Justin asked hopefully, remembering his experience with the tire.

"We do have a coupon with Groupon or LivingSocial if you happen to have one of those," Allison said obligingly.

"Huh? What's Groupon?"

"Groupon.com is a website that has deals for dining, travel, and services. Merchants want to be advertised, and they post deals—generally for half off or better."

"Sounds cool." Justin pulled out his smartphone and purchased a coupon. He then showed the coupon to Allison.

"Wait," said Allison. "This coupon is for $5.00 off an order of $10.00 or more. I won't be able to accept it unless you spend another $1.90—not counting the tax."

"Well, in that case, give me some fresh-baked bread for $2.00," Justin said.

"Your new total is $5.48," Allison said with a smile.

As Justin paid, he asked, "So are you going to take the personal finance class?"

"I don't know," said Allison. "The course seemed good, but the professor was too 'in your face.' By the way, what did he say to you after class?" Allison asked curiously.

"Just two things: One, he liked me for standing up for that guy in our class and he wants me to take the class, and, two, something about things not always being what they seem and that in order to get gold, I need to do things that most people don't know how to do, or where to look—or something like that," Justin responded.

"Hmmm," said Allison. "Have you found any gold?" she asked with a smile.

"Not unless you count the student housing and the FAFSA money and the scholarship," Justin responded.

"Maybe," said Allison with a brief pensive look. "Take care."

"You, too," said Justin, making way for the next customer. Justin sat at a table and ate his food. *She was nice,* he thought, and then as he sat down he realized *she never said she would be taking the class. She's a tricky one.*

Justin had to rush to his next class. At 1 p.m. he had only 30 minutes including travel time to meet with the financial counselor.

School Financial Counselors Can Show Options

Justin met with the counselor, Frank Brown, a few minutes after his appointment time.

"I'd like to know about getting a student loan."

"Have you applied with the FAFSA, the Free Application for Federal Student Aid?" Mr. Brown asked.

"Yes, I got half tuition plus $100."

"Half tuition?" Mr. Brown asked with a tone of curiosity. "How much do your parents earn?"

"Well, my dad did make a lot more," Justin answered, "but just as I left for college, he had to take a 60% pay cut to avoid a layoff. My mom doesn't have a job."

"Hmm." Mr. Brown said. "You may not be aware of it, but due to the changes in circumstance and household income, you might qualify for an increase. What I need you to do is fill out what is called a 'Special Circumstances Application.' You can describe what happened and we will try to request an increase."

"Okay," Justin said, happy to hear he might get additional money.

"Let's fill out the 'Special Circumstances Form,' now," Mr. Brown said, handing it to Justin.

Justin quickly completed the form, and Mr. Brown added the information to Justin's FAFSA profile. The revised profile resulted in Justin getting a full Pell Grant to cover the entire cost of tuition.

"Now that we have that taken care of, do you have any scholarships?" Mr. Brown asked.

"Just one for $120 for books," Justin answered.

"Have you applied to any other scholarships?"

"Yes, I applied for one scholarship, and I'll apply for two more by Saturday. One was with my major, one from Fastweb, and the last is the general scholarship on campus."

"Are you married or the father of any children?"

"No."

"Are you presently employed, and if so, how many hours per week are you working?"

"I have a job as a lab aid. I'm working 15–20 hours a week."

"Do you have any other debts, such as credit cards?"

"No."

"Are your parents claiming you as a dependent, or are you being helped with tuition by them in any way?"

"No to both questions—especially after the pay reduction."

"Look, a lot of students think that they need a student loan because that's what everyone else is doing, but by the sound of things, you already have tuition covered and a job. Even though your parents aren't helping you, you seem to already have most of your expenses covered. I would have pointed you to first apply to FAFSA, check with your department and the campus scholarship fund, and consider getting a student job—but you have already done all of that. Why do you need a loan?"

Justin thought about it for a moment. It surprised him that the counselor wasn't trying to sell him any student loans.[15] With the perspective offered by the counselor, the nagging pit in his gut that had accompanied Justin for days was gone.

"You can always come back next semester and apply for a student loan," Mr. Brown said, "but if you don't get a student loan this semester, you can save yourself one extra semester of future payments that you don't need. Some students say that they need a loan, but many of them are just too scared or lazy to go and get a job to pay for school or rent. You are one of the most prepared students I have

---

15 This may not be the case with all counselors.

seen as a freshman; if you keep applying to more scholarships you will be fine. Who taught you to do all of this?"

"A lot of people have helped, plus a teacher required some of it as an assignment."

"You should thank that teacher. Student loans can be helpful to some students—but very rarely do I find that students actually need them. They can also hurt your financial future. Why sign up for additional debt?"

"Good question," Justin responded.

Justin thanked Mr. Brown and then ran to class. He was ecstatic: his tuition was covered.

At work, he decided that he was going to spend all of his time there applying for scholarships that had deadlines within the next two weeks. The counselor was right: he may not get every scholarship he applied for, but at least by applying he improved his chances of getting some cash.

The only teacher who had even taken note of Justin was Mr. Christensen. *Since I'm a freshman, who else but Professor Christensen would write me a letter of recommendation? But he'd probably scoff at my request for help,* Justin thought to himself. *Well, there is that rule about helping when asked for help—maybe he'd write a letter?* He didn't have time to ask another teacher. It was Friday, the assignment was due Saturday, and the deadline for all the scholarships was Monday. Justin decided a straightforward positive approach might be best for someone as grumpy as the professor.

Dear Professor Christensen,

You may not believe this, but I've already done most of your assignments. I applied with the FAFSA and received full tuition after I met with a counselor. I received a book scholarship from my dad's work for $120. And I was able to get some great advice on what to avoid with student housing by talking to the housing department. Thanks to your assignment, I found a really good deal—and close to campus—that I am renting for a modest price.

I want to apply for the campus general scholarship and I need a letter of recommendation from a teacher. I am a freshman, and since you are the only teacher who even knows who I am, I am asking you for a letter of recommendation. (Just as a reminder, you spoke with me after class on Wednesday and said that you wanted me to take the class.) I am asking if you'd send a letter of recommendation to the Scholarship Department on my behalf. It needs to be received by Monday. I can submit my scholarship application prior to that, and the department staff will wait for your letter to arrive. I will submit my part of the application this afternoon.

Justin then provided the professor with the Scholarship Department's email address, his student number, and a copy of the information from the website about the scholarship, and closed his note with his own contact information.

Justin hoped that Professor Christensen would be empathetic and write a nice letter of recommendation for him. *Well, even if he blows me off, I'll really be no worse off than I am now.*

Starting Tips for Writing Essays

Justin spent the rest of the day at work and doing some readings for homework. When he got a moment, he began an application for the general campus scholarship; this scholarship had one of the nearest deadlines. The application on the website turned out to be a very lengthy one. Justin was asked to write three 250- to 400-word essays on the topics of his leadership abilities, the reasons he needed a scholarship, and someone who had inspired him.

Justin knew the dangers of typing into a browser form; he'd lost papers because of an online glitch. Instead, he typed his essays into MS Word and copied and pasted them onto the scholarship application. Thankfully, the lab was really slow after 3:30 p.m. *After all,* Justin thought, *it is Friday.*

The scholarship application took him about an hour, but he finally finished and submitted it. He saved a screenshot and submitted it on the class website. He went to his email account and composed an email to Professor Christensen, attaching the screenshot of the confirmation to the email he had sent earlier and then added, "I just submitted my application. To fulfill the requirements, I need a letter of recommendation from a teacher." Justin wrote.

He then decided to write the 500-word essay for the scholarship from his department, just in case Professor Christensen didn't respond favorably to his request for help, or in case the professor discredited Justin's effort because of "not doing all of the requirements." Justin could see Professor Christensen taunting him for that very reason.

Justin took out the pages Bob had given him. The topic was 'Why I Chose My Major.' *Well, if I get the scholarship,* Justin mused, *that's a dollar per word.* He wanted to be done with the scholarship application, so he composed it quickly and did a spell check. Upon finishing, he submitted his essay, saved a screenshot of the confirmation, and submitted the screenshot to the class website.

"Done!" Justin said to himself. He was glad it was Friday and hoped to get a little break from homework. He looked for events going on at campus later that night.

Chapter 4: Principles and Suggestions

1. Complete and submit your FAFSA first because that is a requirement [or prerequisite] for many scholarships.

    a.   Go to www.fafsa.ed.gov and fill out an application.

    b.   The FAFSA application takes at least 3–14 business days to be processed AFTER submitting all your information.

2. Apply to as many scholarships as you can. Scholarships can stack, meaning that once tuition has been covered, you may get to keep the remaining money as long as you abide by the parameters of each scholarship. If you don't apply, you cannot get the scholarships.

a. Apply to at least two scholarships every week.

b. If you can, apply for 20 to 50 scholarships over the course of the semester. That may seem like a lot, but it really is just two or three applications a week. It gets easier over

c. The advantage in doing this early is that as the semester continues, you will get busier. Take the time to do it now.

3. Willingness to take just a few extra steps can make a big difference. If there is something that allows you a big payoff, using honorable means, then, by all means, do it. You will be no worse off if you don't get it than you are now, but if you *do* get it, you will be a lot better off. By all means, try.

4. Use Groupon.com or similar sites to get discounts at venues or for services you use.

Chapter 4: Assignments

Get the free workbook at *www.FindingCollegeCash.com/FreeWB*

1. Apply at *www.fafsa.gov*. If you have any questions, please see the College Financial Aid Department.

2. Check for scholarships wherever you can. Apply early.

3. In the workbook, fill out the "True Hourly Wage."

4. In the workbook, read "Basic Essay Tips"

Chapter 4: Warnings and What to Avoid

1. Justin earned money and then treated himself with food. It is good to celebrate the victories—just keep them in balance. The point is to do more than just break-even; it is to grow your money.

2. Student loans are permanent. Right now, unless legislation changes, even if you declare bankruptcy, become ill, or otherwise cannot pay, the loans are NOT going away. They are VERY financially binding.

3. The FAFSA will take longer to be approved than it did in the story. Keep in mind that it takes 3–14 business days.

4. Don't apply for a student loan if you don't need it. You are just costing yourself money.

Chapter 5
Is it Worth It?

Justin got up Saturday morning and read, and then went for a run. When he got back, he found Dave in the kitchen in his pajamas. Dave grinned. "So today's the big moving day, huh?!"

"Yeah," Justin said, "I'll be calling the guys at the house a little bit later, and then I'll move my stuff over."

Justin and Dave chatted a bit more before he packed up his stuff. He figured that 10:00 would be a good time to call the guys at his new place.

"Um, could you come at 4:00 p.m. today?" asked Nate, Justin's new roommate. "A bunch of us are going mountain biking mid-day."

"I guess that would work," Justin said.

Later that day, Justin moved in. At about 7:30 that night, when he was still getting situated, Nate came in and said, "Here's the password to our internet service."

At the mention of "service," Justin remembered his third assignment that he had meant to do earlier: He needed to create a plan for where to give 10% of his income and how he would give at least one hour of unpaid service each week. And he needed to have the plan submitted before 8:00 p.m.

"Real quick," Justin said, "I just remembered that I need to get on the internet and submit an assignment before 8:00 to have it count." He had a mental image of Professor Christensen throwing him out of his class for not finishing his last assignment.

Giving 10% was not that hard. Justin long ago was taught the importance

of tithing to his church. The service part of the assignment was a bit more difficult since he didn't know where he could serve.

Justin consulted his roommates. "Does anyone have some ideas about where
I could do an hour of service weekly? I'm trying to complete an assignment."

His roommates suggested: "Why don't you come and sing with us at an
old folks' home? We do that every Sunday." "How about volunteering at the
University Service Center?" "Maybe you could tutor someone."

Justin decided that he would write down singing at the old folks' home
and volunteering at the University Service Center. He put his plan together,
along with the mention of tithing, and hit "submit." The time was 7:56 p.m. He
had made it! Now, all he had to do was show up in class at 7:00 a.m. Monday
morning. He had done a lot of work just to get accepted into a class. It had
better be worth it! He felt confident though. He was apparently going to get a
lot out of the class, based on what he'd already learned from these assignments.

A New Day—A Metaphor for Change

On Monday, Justin arrived at the classroom at 6:55 a.m. As he walked in, he
saw some students leaving the room, in a hurry. He went into the classroom
and read on the chalkboard:

> *The class location has been changed to the Jones Building, room
> 455. This is also in your email, sent this morning at 6:30 a.m. You
> must be in the room in the Jones Building by no later than 7:05 a.m.
> Please note the camera, which is to make sure that you did, in fact,
> come by 7 a.m.*
>
> *—Professor Christensen*
> *P.S. Take a map with you and an assignment page.*

Stationed above the chalkboard was a circular camera that Justin had
not noticed before. He checked his email on his smartphone to make sure

this was not a joke and, sure enough, Professor Christensen's message was there. On the table below the chalkboard was a stack of campus maps, as well as pieces of paper with blanks on them, marked like a game of Hangman.

—— —— —— —— —— —— —— —— —— —— —— —— ——

Justin now understood why the other students were in a hurry. He picked up a map and a pink sheet of paper and started a fast-paced walk to the Jones Building, the next building over. When he got inside the Jones Building, he ran up the four flights of stairs and entered the appointed classroom at 7:02. He saw written on the chalkboard:

"The fourth letter of the first word is "A." Meet us for class at the Smith Building, near the plaque at the northeast entrance. You have until 7:09 a.m. to get there."

I was just at *the Smith Building.* Shaking his head, Justin marked his paper:

—— —— —— A —— —— —— —— —— —— —— —— —— ——

When Justin arrived at the appointed location, he read the words engraved on the stone plaque: "Our Heritage Is to Move Forward Boldly in Our Cause. —Albert H. Smith" Attached to the plaque, on bright pink paper, was a note, which read:

The second letter of the second word is the last letter of the phrase on your paper. You need to go to the Jones Building, room 102. You must be there by 7:14 a.m. Please note the camera.

Justin looked up and saw a security camera positioned right at the plaque. *Why can't we just get all of the letters at the same building?* Justin thought to himself. He marked his paper.

—— —— —— A —— —— —— —— —— —— —— —— —— E

Justin kept getting directed to go to and from the Jones and Smith Buildings—back and forth. One time he went to a vending machine, another time to a campus statue, and another time to a janitorial closet. Each time, Justin had to cross between the two buildings. He was getting tired of just going back and forth. When he went to one building, he briefly looked around and tried to see any other clues, but they were too well hidden.

His paper now read:

$$\underline{\ \ } \underline{\ \ } \ \underline{C} \ \underline{A} \ \underline{\ \ } \ \underline{E} \ \underline{\ \ \ \ \ } \ \underline{\ \ } \ \underline{A} \ \underline{\ \ } \ \underline{R} \ \underline{A} \ \underline{\ \ } \ \underline{E}$$

He was on his way to the Smith Building, and he had to be there by 7:39. He had saved some time by running, and it was now 7:30. He began to wonder if Professor Christensen was really watching the cameras, or if the students were making fools of themselves going back and forth.

He found the next few letters. Now he had:

$$\underline{E} \ \underline{\ \ } \ \underline{C} \ \underline{A} \ \underline{\ \ } \ \underline{E} \ \underline{\ \ \ \ \ } \ \underline{A} \ \underline{T} \ \underline{R} \ \underline{A} \ \underline{\ \ } \ \underline{E}$$

Justin didn't really have time to guess at the missing letters. The times were getting shorter now, and he had to go to the locations anyway to get the next letter.

After a few more letters, he had:

$$\underline{E} \ \underline{\ \ } \ \underline{C} \ \underline{A} \ \underline{P} \ \underline{E} \ \underline{\ \ \ \ } \ \underline{R} \ \underline{A} \ \underline{T} \ \underline{R} \ \underline{A} \ \underline{C} \ \underline{E}$$

He figured out the word "escape," he had "rat race," and he guessed at possibilities for the middle word, such as "my," or "this," or even "the," but he needed to keep going between the Smith and Jones Buildings. He had shaved about fifteen minutes off his time. Justin then saw a guy with a paper similar to his, who stopped him.

"Hey, I don't know where the fountain is that Professor Christensen was talking about," the guy said.

The fountain was two clues back. Justin wondered if he should help this guy, or not. After all, Justin had found these letters *himself*. He then remembered the rule, "When asked for help, we help."

"The fountain is around the corner, and off to the left," Justin said with a smile. "You'll still need to show up, as there's a camera on the fountain."

"Thanks," said the guy, and he took off running, as did Justin—but in the opposite direction.

Justin found the "S" in escape at the next clue. He then found the word "the" at the next clue. Finally, Justin came to a room that had a note written on the blackboard: "Look at the answer sheet sideways." Justin turned his assignment sheet to the side. Toward the bottom, in a small font, he was directed to an upper room that was part of the Smith Building; he had to be there by 8:29 a.m. He had plenty of time to arrive, as it was only 7:55.

Escaping the Rat Race

At the door stood Professor Christensen with a smile on his face. He greeted Justin warmly and said: "Mr. Murray, I'm so glad to see you. You obviously learned that things are not always as they seem. Come on in and have some bagels and orange juice. You might like the show, as well. By the way, how did you like the rat race—showing up at times required by someone else, always going back and forth, and trying to 'keep up with the Joneses'?"

"It was kind of frustrating and I felt like I was wasting my time, just going back and forth. When I finally got to the end and found that I could have accomplished the same thing with less time and effort, I was annoyed," Justin said.

"I agree. Here's a dollar for your time," Professor Christensen said as he handed Justin a dollar bill.

Justin looked at the dollar and felt it really wasn't worth his time and effort. In fact, it was almost insulting, but he took the dollar anyway. He entered the room and saw several students, many of whom he didn't recognize from the first day of class. Also, several students from the first day were not present; apparently, they had decided to not take the class. Projected onto a big screen were eight images, with a clock in the bottom corner. Justin saw the original classroom, the fountain, the plaque, and several other locations. He watched as his fellow students ran back and forth.

Justin then saw Allison. She was here! Justin felt secretly happy. He looked at the table near her and saw that there were whole-wheat bagels, cream cheese, and bottles of orange juice. He headed over; she was eating a bagel.

"How's it going?" Allison asked him.

"Okay. How did you beat me here?" Justin asked with a smile, grabbing a bagel.

"I saw Professor Christensen's email, and started before you did," Allison responded. "I noticed the small print when I stopped to tie my shoe. Professor Christensen did a good job making the clues go in a circle so that students couldn't find the other clues. It was kind of funny and sad to watch everyone run the rat race. Thanks for the tip the other day. I was questioning whether I wanted to be in this class, but when I heard about your results and the tip about looking for gold, I figured I should at least try. It turns out that Professor Christensen wasn't what he seemed at first, either. He seems really nice."

"It surprised me, when I came in, how friendly he was. What did you think of his rat race?" Justin asked.

"It seemed a lot like my job, a lot of effort and little pay," Allison said. This got Justin thinking about work and how he seemed to be going back and forth—always on someone else's schedule.

"Hey—that rude guy is coming in," Allison said as she pointed towards the screen.

Justin turned and saw Malcolm (the spikey-haired guy who had argued with Professor Christensen during the first class) on the screen, coming up to the room. Justin looked at the clock and saw that it was 8:27 a.m. Malcolm entered with a scowl on his face.

Professor Christensen closed the door to the room and announced, "Everyone who would like me to sign an add/drop card may come up front, and we'll get those signed so that you can take off. All that will be left is for you to go to the registrar's office and drop off the cards.

"What was it like going back and forth between the Smith and Jones Buildings?" Professor Christensen asked.

"Awful."

"I felt like I was getting nowhere."

"I was annoyed until I saw the answer written on the side of the sheet, then I realized it was a game you were playing."

"I thought it was ridiculous."

"This is how life often expects us to live our lives. Going here, there, and everywhere on other people's schedules," Professor Christensen said. "I want to teach you all how to live your life in a way that allows you to choose what you do with your time. Sometimes it is necessary to run the rat race until you learn how to escape, but you can try to make it a short race.

"T. Harv Eker in his book *Your Millionaire Mind* tells how, in his mid-twenties, he wanted to go into the pie business but didn't know much about that industry. He got a job as a pie shelf stocker and learned the business; he learned about the suppliers, the customers, the products, and ultimately, he learned that he didn't want to be in the pie business. He realized that this type of work was not fulfilling to him. He was paid to come to this realization.

"A few days after he quit, he was approached by a former co-worker about going into business in the fitness industry. He also investigated this industry and found it to be an emerging opportunity. He really enjoyed this line of work. This opportunity led to a new career path for him and ultimately made him a millionaire. T. Harv Eker was in the rat race to learn how to get out. Sometimes it is necessary to be in the rat race, but only as long as you are looking for ideas or gaining capital. We will talk more about practical steps on how to get out of the race later in the semester. In the race that I had you participate in today, all of you carried the answers with you, but you didn't know it. You can achieve the same results a lot quicker if you just learn how and where to look.

"If you learn to do things just a little differently, you can have and do things that other people only dream of. You don't have to be *ten* times better, just a *little* bit better. In the Olympics, the first-, second-, third-, and fourth-place finishers could all be within half a second of each other. Now, the first-place winner is not 10 times better—just a few milliseconds better—but he or she gets roughly 10 times the amount of fame that the second-place winner gets because book publishers, talk shows, and company sponsors line up to interview and reward the winner. In turn, the second-place finisher gets about 10 times more reward than the third-place finisher. As for the fourth-place finisher, he or she might get an article written in a hometown newspaper, along with some local and fleeting fame, but that doesn't begin to equal the reward of the first-place winner for being just a little bit better. That is all it takes, not a huge amount of effort, just a little bit of directed effort. Actually, it can be even less effort than what you normally would make but it is focused on achieving certain results. Later in the semester, I am going to teach you some business concepts that, if applied, may allow you to never have to enter the rat race and to choose to be free to live your life.[16]

"In this class, I am going to teach you both how to earn money and how to manage money so that you can avoid student loans and common financial traps college students fall into—if you follow the principles. I call it *C-A-S-H, or Controlling expenses, Amplifying Income, Setting and achieving goals, and Having systems*."

Professor Christensen continued, "I want you all to know that who I was *pretending* to be last class and who I *really* am are completely different.

---

16 For more information on this see: Finding College Cash: Business by the author.

In fact, when Mr. Murray, here, called me on my ploy, I had a hard time keeping a straight face and not laughing. As an apology for acting like a jerk, I am taking you bowling for the next class. It will be completely free to you if you get to the campus lanes in the Student Center by 7 a.m. on Wednesday; otherwise, you will pay $12 for the lane and the shoes, plus a late fee."

There were expressions of excitement.

Your True Hourly Rate of Pay

After letting the excitement wear down, Professor Christensen continued speaking. "Before you leave to take your add/drop card to the registrar's office, I want to commend each and every one of you. To get here, each of you had to face the challenges of the unknown, and you did so with some effort. Some of you have told me that because you took action, you were awarded money through a Pell Grant or a scholarship, or you even saved money on housing. Stop and think about it. If you were to spend forty hours applying to scholarships and other forms of financial aid and received just $1,000 from any of those sources, it would still equal $25 per hour. What's more is that you didn't have to pay payroll taxes on this $25 per hour rate. You still will need to declare the money on your income taxes at the end of the year, but tell me honestly, what job could you get as a student with no degree, limited work experience, and only a small handful of skills? Many of you will find that you will end up making closer to $200 per hour if you consistently apply for scholarships and other financial resources."

Twenty-five dollars an hour for forty hours of work?! Justin thought. *I spent about fifteen hours and received much more than $1,000.* Justin realized that he had already been paid over $400 per hour from the scholarships he won, the Pell Grant, and the savings on a room to rent. *Holy smokes! Professor Christensen was right; I didn't have time to waste. I earned more with this than with my job.*

"Even if you did not get any money yet," Professor Christensen said, interrupting Justin's thoughts, "keep going. The first time you got on a bicycle you probably weren't that great at it, but with consistent effort, you can now ride a bicycle without too much thought. The same goes for this class. You will get better as you go along. The secret is to take advantage of almost any opportunity available to you. Twenty scholarships worth an average of $1,000 each is $20,000. There are some students who make over $1,000,000 applying to financial aid; they pay for school and pocket the rest. This is why I am requiring you apply for two scholarships every week. By the end of the semester, you will have applied for at least thirty scholarships, and some of you will apply to more. What is *your* goal for how many scholarships you are going to apply for this semester?"

Forty scholarships or more, AND apply to at least $100,000 worth of scholarships, Justin thought.

After You Are Awarded Any Money

"For those of you who did get a scholarship," Professor Christensen said, "I want you to write a thank-you letter to the scholarship committee and donors. You want these people to remember you and feel that they made a good choice in picking you as the winner. In some cases, you may be eligible in six months or a year to apply again and this can help you get a renewal. While I will not track this portion of the assignment, I want you to send a thank-you letter or note to anyone, or any entity, who pays for any portion of your schooling—including your parents if they help you."

"Finally," Professor Christensen said, "I am requesting that you keep track of how much money you get from what source. You may also want to keep track of any scholarships that you were a finalist in or made any cut. There are two reasons for keeping track of the money you earned: One, you will need this information for taxes; I can guarantee that the committees for scholarships, grants, and other resources will keep track of awarding you the money. If you fail to report this as income, you will be responsible to the IRS and state governments. Two, on your résumé, even if you didn't win any money, you can state 'finalist for XYZ scholarship.' Obviously, it is better if you won, but even if you just say finalist or 'first-tier,' this gives you a measure of implied credibility."

Malcolm blurted out, "Excuse me, Professor. Why are you having us work so hard, and do so many things after we already received the money? Why not take the money and run?"

Professor Christensen gave a slight chuckle and said "At first it would seem like that would be sensible, but remember, I don't give assignments just to keep you busy with tasks. I am actually making your life easier. If you become known as a good, honorable person, this can translate into better opportunities for you. You may be surprised to what extent people remember you when you later need something like a letter of recommendation from them. Next, if you don't keep track, then on your tax return you will be guessing on the amount of money you earned. You could be audited and fined or—in extreme cases—charged with tax evasion. Last, trying to remember all of your accomplishments is hard for résumés and other applications.

"Let's save the rest of the lesson for another day. Go to the registrar's office to submit your add/drop card to be in the class."

Cash-Strapped—Planning in Advance

Justin went to the office to turn in his add/drop card. There was a line, but Justin was happy to wait to get this class—plus he was going bowling. While Justin waited he started thinking. *Well, I was certainly wrong about Professor Christensen. I guess that was why his face was twitching the other day; he was trying not to laugh. I'm surprised I didn't realize it. Things are not always what they seem, and to find gold, I have to be willing to do what other people aren't willing to do.*

When he got to the window a female student attendant took his add/drop card. "It looks like you have enough credits to be on full-time student status. Today is the deadline to pay tuition." She gave the cost.

"Did my Pell Grant come in?"

After looking up Justin's profile, she said, "The registrar's office can only see if your tuition has been paid. The tuition office can tell you the specifics. However, it looks like your tuition has been covered. You're all set for this semester."

"Great!" Justin said, then turned and left.

His other classes went well, but in each class he was assigned more readings and homework. Wondering how he was going to do everything, he raced home to grab some lunch before work and was handed some mail by one of his roommates. He stuffed the mail in his backpack, quickly grabbed a PB&J sandwich, and ran to work.

After helping a couple of students in the lab, he opened up his mail. The first letter was from the University Scholarship Department. He was excited all over again! Justin opened the envelope and read the letter:

Dear Mr. Murray,

Thank you for applying for the campus general scholarship. We regret to inform you that you were not selected for the general scholarship as an incoming freshman.

Best of luck to you. We encourage you to apply again next year.

Sincerely,
Syracuse State University Scholarship Department

Justin was disappointed. *That stinks!* Justin thought. *I spent about three hours on that essay and the revision time. I was kind of hoping to get at least a $100 scholarship. What kind of result is that?* Miffed, he started thinking that he had wasted his time. *What a waste! What good does applying for scholarships do if I don't get anything from it?* The next envelope was from his cell phone provider. Justin knew that it had been forwarded by his mom; it was his monthly bill. He put the rest of his mail aside and looked at his bank account.

Justin had not yet received a paycheck. From the nearly $1,000 with which he had started, he had paid off his credit card. Between the deposit for his rent, the monthly rent due, the new tire, books, gasoline, and food, he was down to $108.13.

Justin cringed. While it was true that he didn't have to pay tuition because of the Pell Grant, he was essentially broke. He wouldn't have much money left: the cell phone bill would be about $75. He wouldn't get his first check for two weeks—one more week of work, and another of processing. *How am I going to live for two weeks on about $20?* Justin didn't have an answer. *Maybe I do need that student loan.*

Justin was too upset to do any homework. He decided to check his email. Amid other emails, there was one from Syracuse State University, with the subject "Urgent Attention Requested." Justin clicked on the email; it read (a made-up scenario):

Dear Mr. Murray,[17]

The school has received your application for a Pell Grant. While you have been approved, there has been a delay in the government's release date. Because of this year's early add/drop deadline, the funds will not be received until after school starts.

You will still need to pay your tuition in full by the add/drop deadline. If you need a temporary loan, please see the tuition office prior to the add/drop deadline. Students who fail to pay for tuition by the add/drop deadline will be dropped from classes this semester.

Sincerely,
Syracuse State University Department of Finance

---

17 This scenario is made up. Check with your school about processes. Please forgive the author for adding some excitement to a book about money.

Panic engulfed Justin. *The office will close in ten minutes; there is no way I can make it there by 5:00 p.m. to get a loan and pay for tuition. Am I going to be dropped as a student? Why did the person at the registrar's office tell me my tuition had been covered when it really hadn't? Could I petition for an extension?*

Justin felt alone and for one of the first times in his life, he was scared of what financial problems could do to his future. The prerequisites for freshmen in his major were only offered in the fall. While he could take alternative classes next semester, he would still have to wait to take his major's prerequisites next fall.

Justin didn't know what to do. He felt sick. He quickly locked his computer and decided that he would try to run to the tuition office to plead his case. As he got up, he noticed his pile of mail. Below his credit card bill, there were several other envelopes. One was a junk mail offer for a credit card. At the bottom of the pile, he saw a cream-colored envelope. Justin grabbed all the mail to shove into his bag but stopped when he saw the cream-colored envelope's return address: the Office of Prestigious Scholarships. Justin opened the envelope as he was half running down the hall.

The letter began with "Congratulations!" He had been awarded a four-year full-tuition scholarship as long as he maintained a 3.4 GPA, starting this semester! It was called the Gordon and Betty Osborn Scholarship, and it was given only to incoming freshman.

Justin was astounded. *Holy cow!* He couldn't believe it. He had gotten a scholarship and not just any scholarship—a prestigious one! Justin felt like jumping over the moon.

Thank you, God! Thank you! Thank you!

Justin hadn't been this ecstatic for a long time. He felt like he had as a kid when he got a bicycle that he wanted at Christmas.

Maybe that is what the registrar's office lady meant about my tuition being covered. Justin returned to the computer lab. Some of the students looked at him inquisitively.

Justin quickly logged into his computer, then to the student portal, and went to the tuition payments. Tuition had been covered by the scholarship. The Pell Grant was shown as pending. He also saw the $120 from his dad's employer.

With the Pell Grant and the scholarships, thousands of dollars were now his. Justin realized that he had been paid over $800 an hour. He couldn't help thinking, *I'm rich! I wonder if I'll get both scholarships? I got double tuition, without working for it.*

Chapter 5: Principles and Suggestions

1. Focus on doing things slightly differently; that will bring you wealth. Building wealth or paying for college often doesn't require massive changes, just slight changes.

2. Keeping up with the Joneses (buying what you don't need) is a dangerous game. Spend money on what is truly important to you; avoid the rest. Stay in the rat race only to learn to get out.

3. Be willing to give service to those around you. Giving of yourself allows you to build relationships and often, if you teach another, you gain more understanding yourself.

4. While it is possible to pay for college with just one resource, you can greatly improve your chances of paying for college without incurring debt if you use a combination of resources. If you would like some help learning to pay for college, please visit *www.FindingCollegeCash.com/FreeVideo*, where you can get a free video course on how to get help paying for college.

Chapter 5: Assignments

Get the free workbook at *www.FindingCollegeCash.com/FreeWB*

1. Write a form letter that you can use to thank donors and scholarship committees.

2. Decide what your goal is when applying for scholarships. Fill out the section in the workbook called "Scholarship Goals."

3. Read and use the section in the workbook called "Expressing Gratitude." Use the template to send thank-you letters.

4. Complete the section on "Your Emergency Fund" in the workbook.

Chapter 5: Warnings and What to Avoid

1. Don't assume that if you fail to manage your resources, you will have money available to you when you need it.

2. Please DON'T do what Justin did and wait until college starts. Yes, it can be done, but waiting until the last minute can cause a lot of anxiety and even desperation. The sooner you start, the more options you will have.

Chapter 6
Money Seeds and Writing Right

Justin was really glad he had enrolled in Professor Christensen's class. He was excited to go bowling, and he was beginning to see the point of many of the lessons that Professor Christensen was teaching—both directly and indirectly. Plus, the professor was very nice after all—he even handled Malcolm with courtesy.

Focus on What Matters

Wednesday came. Professor Christensen had reserved the entire bowling alley for the class at an hour when it was not usually available to most students. At 7 a.m., the alley was usually closed. Justin really enjoyed bowling with the class. He got a 147 and "just happened" to be on Allison's team. After bowling, the class went to the lobby.

Professor Christensen addressed them. "Did you know that Jeff Olson, in his book *The Slight Edge*, said that the average millionaire's bowling score is under a hundred? His point was that you should focus on what gives you freedom—that is, earning and managing your money—instead of focusing exclusively on things that have little return on investment, such as bowling. Focus on what matters to you, and let the rest be as it is. If your goal is to be a professional bowler, do that and be the best you can be. However, if your goal is to be wealthy, then focus on integrity and correct principles of building wealth. Let the unimportant stuff fall away and don't worry that you are not the best."

A guy Justin hadn't yet met raised his hand and asked: "Are you trying to tell us to not sweat the small things?"

"Exactly! Focus on what really matters to you."

"Class, you don't need to eliminate all social events, but unless your goal is to become a professional bowler or a bowling instructor, you shouldn't put time and energy into bowling, because that will offer little reward. Don't worry if you don't do too well at unimportant things. Focus on what it is you truly want for yourself. Have fun as you attend college; however, by doing things just slightly different than most people, you can have ten times the rewards that they have." With a smile, the professor added, "By focusing on gaining and managing money, you can *first* achieve financial independence and *then* go bowling—or do whatever you wish—without the worries of the obligations that most people are faced with, day in and day out, and especially without the debt."

Justin realized the point of going bowling: *By focusing on what matters most, people can have, do, and be more than they otherwise could. He didn't need to eliminate fun—just choose what was important to him and focus on that.*

"Now, this being said," Professor Christensen again interrupted Justin's thoughts, using a compelling voice that invited attention, "even if you choose bowling as your focus, I can show you how you can do more with bowling than you have ever thought possible and build wealth in the process, but this will require you to do things in a new way that most people don't think about. There are infinite ways to make money, but if you follow a few key principles, getting wealth will be a lot easier and faster."

Justin could tell that Professor Christensen was really passionate about what he was teaching.

Money Seeds—Paying It Forward

"Let me share an analogy that might help you and that has at least three applications," said the professor. "Let's imagine that in the Philippines there's a massive hurricane that wipes out all of the crops in early spring. Two Americans go over to help as volunteers: One is from a major city and has never been to a farm or seen plants grow, and the other is from the country. As the Philippine lands are salvaged, some bags of rice are found that are unspoiled and intact. The country volunteer takes 10% of the bags of rice and, with the help of the people, starts planting the rice in the ground. Now, the city volunteer would question the sanity of the other volunteer. 'What are you doing?' the city volunteer says. 'These people *need* this rice; they're starving. Why are you just wasting it, throwing it into the ground?' The country volunteer says, 'I know. That's why I'm planting it now. The only way to increase what they have in the future is to *plant* this rice. For every grain that is planted, 20 to 300 more grains will grow from it. By putting at least 10% of this rice into the ground, we're providing for the people *so* much more rice than the 10% we're planting.'"

Professor Christensen then asked the class, "Who do you think was doing more to help the people living with the destruction from the hurricane: the volunteer from the city or the one from the country?"

"The one from the country," a girl responded.

"Why?" Professor Christensen asked her and the class.

"Well," the girl began, "the volunteer from the country is giving the people more food and more grain by planting it. He is helping them to rebuild."

"Do you think that to the inexperienced volunteer from the city, the actions seem foolish—I mean, putting stuff in the ground, expecting it to grow?" Professor Christensen asked.

"I suppose so," said another guy in the class, "but that's only because he hasn't seen stuff grow before and has no experience with harvesting crops."

"Very good," said Professor Christensen.

"Wait, that's messed up," said Malcolm. "Why couldn't the people in the story have eaten their rice and waited for other countries to help them out? I mean, they're obviously sending two Americans, why couldn't they have planted the rice and seeds sent from other countries, instead of their own rice? They'd still get crops at the end of the harvest."

"Interesting point, Mr. Fredrickson," said Professor Christensen.

"It's Malcolm," he responded curtly.

"All right, Malcolm, let's look at it. First, they don't know how long other countries will continue to support them, especially if they don't try to support themselves when they have the means. Second, they'll still have to plant something in order to continue to eat, and since those crops take time to grow, if the people wait longer to plant they may not have fully developed rice when they need it."

"*Whatever*! I'd still eat the bags of rice while I had them," Malcolm said. "What good is future rice if everyone is dead?"

Money Seed 1

"It sounds to me as though you can relate more to the volunteer from the city than the one from the country," Professor Christensen said politely in response to this comment. "I want to come to you as an experienced, old farmer who knows how to grow *money*. Money seeds act the same way as the rice in this story, and we need to plant them. How we plant them is by taking 10% of our money and giving it to charities as tithing. Just like planting crops, money crops require seeds. When you plant rice or corn, you first have to give away some of your rice or corn by planting it, but in return at the harvest, you get hundreds of corn kernels returned to you. I can tell you that, from my experience, tithing works.

"Let's consider the facts and evidence. Many of the wealthiest people in the world 10% or more of their money toward tithing. Some of these past and present people are John D. Rockefeller, Henry Ford, Glenn Beck, Bill Gates (both his company and him personally), billionaire David Green, Jon Huntsman, and many more. Mark Victor Hansen repeatedly has said that his book series *Chicken Soup for the Soul* has done as well as it has because at least 10% of the profits from every book are donated to charitable causes. If some of the richest people in history tithe, I suggest you pattern yourselves after them by paying your tithing. *Do they give because they are rich or are they rich because they give?* Think about this, are they rich first or are they willing to give first? I suggest they are rich because they give and follow good principles. Why don't you each decide to do both: follow good principles and pay tithing?

"Many people report that tithing to a cause they believe in increases their appreciation for life and allows them to be more responsible with the rest of their money.

"Back when I was a student and hurting for cash, I would pay my tithing and things worked out—sometimes from unexpected sources. Tithing is a catalyst for good things.

"I realize you are students and may not have much money; I come to you as an old farmer. Plant your money seeds by paying your tithing first and finding at least five hours where you can serve others during the month. Give first to get.

"As a word of caution, many people foolishly say that if they pay their tithing, they will be supported in all their efforts or they can demand a specific degree of prosperity; **this is not true**. We still need to adhere to good principles to claim the blessings. I repeat: tithing is a catalyst when combined with sound principles.

"If any farmer stops obeying correct principles, such as taking care of and watering his crops, and willfully neglects his responsibility, then even if he pays his tithing, it's likely that his crops will wither and die. This doesn't mean that tithing failed. It means that the farmer was not following correct principles."

"Wait! Are you going to make us pay 10% of our money just to complete an assignment?" Malcolm asked with an obvious tone of panic and annoyance.

"I actually thought about it, because I know the benefit of tithing and service," Professor Christensen said with a smile. "However, I believe that for tithing to work you need to choose to do it for yourself. Service is a different matter. I'm going to require four to five hours per month. You need to decide if you want to give your tithing by donating 10% of your income to your church, synagogue, mosque, temple, or a charitable cause that you believe in."

"Enough with the preaching," Malcolm blurted out. "Just tell us how to make money."

Another guy responded more favorably and asked in a positive tone, "Does tithing really work? I mean, if I pay 10% of my money, will prosperity really happen?"

"You still have to adhere to correct principles," Professor Christensen replied, ignoring Malcolm's comment, "and if you do so, and pay your tithing, you will prosper in ways you can't know right now. You don't get to pick what those good things are, or how they come, but they do come. Does anyone have any examples of tithing?" Professor Christensen asked.

Allison quickly responded. "I was once wondering if I should pay tithing when I didn't have a job, but I did it anyway, and the next week I was offered a job."

Justin realized that he had consistently paid his tithing, and he had never starved, but how had tithing helped him? Then he remembered Paul's help with textbooks and all that Paul had taught him, which had saved him some money. Also, he had gotten into this class. "I have always paid my tithing, and my friend showed me how to save money on my school books, and I was given a scholarship—almost by accident. When I think about these events, I really didn't do too much; they just came to me."

"So, you were blessed in ways that you didn't expect but which helped you to gain what you needed to prosper. Is that right?" asked Professor Christensen.

"Yeah," said Justin, becoming more aware of some of the ways he had been blessed on his trip to Syracuse.

"I know that the critic would say, 'Oh, those things came because of the people you knew or what you did. Those events don't really have anything to do with tithing.' However, put it to the test for six months, I say, and you will see a major difference in your life," Professor Christensen said.

"*Now* can we learn about the money stuff?" Malcolm insistently asked.

Professor Christensen replied: "Well, that was some of the most important 'money stuff,' but let me share with you some other ways to look at the rice in the analogy about the Philippines."

"Not more about tithing," Malcolm protested.

"Don't worry Malcolm," Professor Christensen responded sympathetically and with a wry smile, "I have plenty more to teach you about money so you won't run out of things to complain about."

Most of the class chuckled—all but Malcolm.

After the laughter waned, Professor Christensen continued.

Money Seed 2

"Another money seed is paying yourself first. You should put away at least 10% of your money before it goes to bills or fun. You should save up the money first—no debt. In saving up for tuition or rent, you should save more than 10%, and it is possible to have the money for the next semester earned this semester or earlier. This will help you to save literally thousands of dollars by not paying interest and fees. In future classes, we will discuss how to save up for these items.

"When you start working, you will want to follow this pattern in saving for retirement. We will briefly talk about some of the options for retirement later."

Money Seed 3

"The final money seed you will want is saving up for is your dreams. Most people pay for things on credit and then pay for them over and over. Instead, save up for your dreams—most of the time when you save up for them, your dreams are cheaper, or you will find creative ways to make them happen.

"These money seeds are how you should view your after-tax income: 10% to tithing, (at least), 10% to savings, and 10% toward your dreams. Live on the remaining 70%. Because you are in college, you probably should reverse those numbers, live on 30% of your income and put the rest toward school. One of your dreams can be paying for college without student loans and credit card debt."

I know I made this goal before to find a way to pay for college, but breaking down the numbers like that is really helpful. I will pay for college without student loans and credit card debt, Justin thought to himself—a little more resolutely.

"I have an assignment for you that I will email to you tomorrow. It is a project of sorts, so set some time aside to complete it." Professor Christensen continued, "For other principles, we'll have to wait till next time. Class dismissed."

Right after the dismissal, Justin went up to Allison and asked, "Would you like to meet up at the library to work on the assignment and project together?"

"Sure," Allison replied with a little bit of hesitation. "Mind if I invite Maria to come with me?"

"Not a problem," Justin responded coolly. "Does 7 p.m. Thursday sound good?"

"That works. See you then."

Two for one—not bad odds, Justin thought after they parted.

Internship, Scholarship, and Timing Ideas

After Justin had finished work, he went home and found his roommate Nate completing some paperwork. Trying to be friendly, Justin asked, "Whatcha up to?"

"I'm writing some résumés and cover letters for internships I want to be accepted into next semester," Nate said. "I'm looking for an internship that will last through the winter."

"Wait, I thought that internships were in the summer," Justin said, confused.

"That's what most people do," Nate responded. "But that is part of the problem: most people take internships in the summer, so there are fewer available. I've found that many companies are willing to hire interns in the fall and winter months—in fact, it is often easier to get an internship in the fall or winter than in the summer because there's less competition."

"That's good to know."

"Yeah, but as an added bonus, I take classes in the summer. The teachers then tend to eliminate a lot of the busy work that you can sometimes get—either the semesters are shorter or the teachers don't want to spend the time to put the students through the same quantity of assignments, knowing that they'll need to grade the extra homework in their summer break," Nate added with a smile.

Essay Ideas

"Interesting idea," Justin said. "I am going to have to remember that. Just curious, what do you do to help you get noticed as an applicant?"

"Well, I took a class that talked about how to apply to jobs," Nate said. "I learned a good formula to use."

"What's the formula?" Justin asked.

"*Problem + Solution = Measurable Results as a Story*," Nate said.

"What do you mean by that?" Justin asked.

"Organizations love things that are quantified. Let's say that the pastor asks ten people to help clean up and weed the churchyard. The job takes two hours."

Instead of just saying: "I helped clean my church," say something like: "I volunteered as part of a ten-person committee to help make improvements at a local community center by removing debris and improving the landscaping. Our group spent over twenty hours on these improvements, filled two dumpsters with yard debris, and significantly improved the aesthetic appeal of the community center to the over 500 active members who use it."

"Can you see a difference?" Nate asked.

"Yeah, with the first, I really don't know what you did. With the second, I was able to get a really good idea of what you did, while making it seem…well, *important*. Why did you call the church a community center?" Justin asked.

"We live in strange times; people have biases against any mention of God, church, and even family. While I don't agree with that notion, and there have been many improvements in public acceptance of speaking about God, I try to make it something that other people can relate to. I don't need to tell the review board (unless they ask) that the committee was really five members of my family, or that the community center was a church, but I identified the problem, gave solutions, and provided numbers that were measurable—all told as a story. I can do the same thing with school projects, Scouting endeavors, and leadership skills—just don't take it too far; you can over-embellish the story and discredit yourself."

"Wait," Justin said, "I don't want to write that every time I apply for a job."

"Save your work," Nate said. "You can write it once, put it in a file on your computer, and then copy it later. It becomes a matter of which story do I want to use for any given event. One more thing…"

"Yeah, what's that?" Justin asked.

"Something that really helps is if you find out the name of the person or the title of the committee that'll be reviewing your application. So, unless the application requires 'To Whom It May Concern,' don't put that; it is really impersonal and makes the reader feel like he or she is reading a form letter. Say something like 'Dear Members of the A.P.T. Company Review Board' or 'Dear Mr. Jones.' It is so much nicer than a form letter, and shows that you at least have done some research about the organization that you are applying to."

Justin thanked his roommate and left. After the conversation, Justin made a mental note: *I can do that with my scholarships. If I just make a list of stories about my life experiences and save them, I can speed up how long it will take me to apply for scholarships. That was really good to hear about the names as well. If I spend less time writing a scholarship essay, I can spend a little more time researching who will actually see my scholarship applications.*

Essay Preparation — Make Note of Your Activities

The next day after class, Professor Christensen sent out an email. It read:

Dear Class,

Thank you so much for coming bowling with me. I really enjoyed getting to know each of you.

Go do two activities that are fun. You must be prepared to tell the class how you found free activities. You must invite a group of at least three people. TV, movies, and video games are not allowed. Be creative and have fun, but find ways that you can have fun for free with other people.

Have a great weekend!

—Professor Christensen

Justin was surprised! That was Professor Christensen's homework: Go have fun. He liked his class more and more.

Justin went to the designated spot on campus, just south of the library, and saw Allison, Maria, and Tyler. Maria had invited him along, too. That was okay with Justin, although he was mildly disappointed to lose his two-to-one ratio with the girls.

You Benefit by Helping Others

They went into the library. The others were surprised when Justin told them about the homework assignment; none of them had read it yet. Tyler insisted on checking his email to make sure Justin wasn't just trying to have a good time at his expense. When he saw it was the truth, they started discussing some of their ideas.

Maria spoke first. "Hey, do you remember when we went bowling and Professor Christensen mentioned that millionaires don't focus on activities that don't have a payoff? Maybe this is really more of a test to see what we learned and if we will follow principles. Well, I suggest that we go find someone to serve for one of the activities. At least that way we can fulfill some of our service requirement—you know, kill two birds with one stone."

They all thought that was a great idea. Ideas flowed back and forth about who they could serve, especially on a Saturday. The first idea was tutoring someone, but they didn't know whom to tutor on such short notice.

Then Tyler suggested that they pick up some trash on campus. But when they looked around, they decided the campus actually looked fairly clean. So *that* didn't work.

Allison asked, "What was that app Professor Christensen told us about?"

"I think it was the JustServe App," Maria responded.

After downloading the app, Allison searched for service activities near their location. "There's a rest home a couple of blocks away from the campus with visiting hours right now. Why don't we go over there?"

Everyone agreed and they walked to the rest home. After checking in, they said that they wanted to visit the residents. The attendant said it would be great. They went from room to room, visiting the residents and asking them how they were doing. The residents' eyes lit up when they saw that somebody was there to see them.

The four students were able to meet a whole lot of different people, and they were even asked to come again. As they were going down the hall, one of the attendants said, "Visiting hours will be ending in about ten minutes. We need to be able to get the residents ready for bed."

So, Justin and the others decided that they would say their final goodbyes. They went in one last room and saw a sweet old lady. She said that her name was Sally. She was sad, but the girls warmed very quickly to her. They asked her how she was doing and how she was feeling, and Sally replied that she was doing all right.

Then an attendant came in and said, "Hi, Sally. How's it going today?"

"Well, much better now that these young people are here," Sally replied with a smile.

"Oh, I'm so glad to see that you're visiting her today," the attendant said to the students.

With notice that their time was up, the four headed for the door in a chorus of goodbyes to Sally.

Justin went home and thought about what they had done. Professor Christensen had given them the charge to have fun, and Justin thought that had been a great activity. Plus, it was an excuse to see Allison.

Justin then remembered that he needed to have two activities. He decided to invite his roommates and some of his neighbors to come play a board game. He finished about an hour later.

Justin finished submitting his weekly scholarship applications from Fastweb and Big Future. He copied his submissions and put the submissions onto the class website.

Writing a Good Essay

Monday in class, Professor Christensen asked everyone to come with him on a field trip. He took them to the campus library, where they went into a classroom with computers for everyone. Professor Christensen had reserved it for the class.

"Okay," Professor Christensen said, "what were some of the free activities you did with your groups of three or more?" The class began to share their activities.

"Played touch football."

"Had a potluck dinner."

"We went to a retirement home."

"Went to a free concert on campus."

"My friends and I played a board game."

"I hope you enjoyed having fun for free," Professor Christensen said. "In today's class, we are going to discuss some tips for essays." There were several students who bemoaned the idea until Professor Christensen reminded them about being positive.

"Let's use everyday experiences to describe your leadership abilities. What you didn't realize was that by gathering a group together to have fun, you were actually being a leader. People often think that they must have huge and monumental types of leadership positions to be a leader; this is inaccurate. Just because someone may be put near the top of an organization does not automatically make him (or her) the leader—that is just a figurehead, such as a family company where the son inherits the father's business. The son may inherit the title but may lack the ability to lead the business. Being a leader means that you provide vision and direction, and influence others to follow you by example, not coercion. There are two things that scholarship committees love to see: one is leadership, and the other is service. This is why I had each of you invite people to participate in a fun activity: I wanted you to all have two examples of leadership; you have examples of service in your weekly hour of service that is part of your grade. We are going to discuss some of the ways to present these attributes and events in essays now."

Professor Christensen turned and wrote on the marker board: "Statement + Problem + Solution = Results as a Story."

Justin remembered part of this equation from his roommate Nate. Justin wondered if there was a correlation.

"Let's take the information from your activities," Professor Christensen said, "and write two short essays. For example, let's start with the football game. That means that you had about ten people, for a small group, or twenty-two for a full-size game. What were some of the details?" Professor Christensen asked the student who had said, 'I played touch football.'

"I invited thirteen people and eleven of them showed up. We played Saturday morning for about an hour and a half."

"Good," Professor Christensen said, "now let's write an essay. I don't know all the details, but I will make them up. Fair enough?"

The student nodded. Professor Christensen continued. "You could write a simple statement saying "'I played football with my friends.' But really that doesn't tell much. Instead, let's use the formula. Statement: 'I have always been a leader.' Let's then use the rest of the formula: 'For example, people in my apartment were wanting to do something fun. I invited thirteen people to come join me for a morning of physical activity participating in flag football.' This is the statement of the problem. Now let's write the solution. 'Eleven of the thirteen people invited attended. I coordinated the location and time, and invited the people; I also presented an idea to divide teams. Everyone agreed, and we divided into teams according to my plan. I suggested to my team that someone else should be the quarterback because he had a better throwing arm. We played a ten-point game that lasted one-and-a-half hours. One of the plays that was my idea led to a touchdown.'"

"Aren't you telling the result, or the 1.5 hours and the number of people that came, instead of the solution?" the student asked.

"Partially correct," Professor Christensen replied. "Part of the result is mixed in the solution, but let me finish."

"Okay."

"The results are both soft and hard results. For example: 'After playing, several people came up and thanked me for inviting them and said that they would like to play again if I ever arranged another game. Since that game, I have invited groups of people and we meet once a week to play. From this experience, I learned true leadership is a state of mind: a willingness to involve others, and provide direction with a common goal.'"

"So the results are the measurements, and the lessons learned?"

"You guessed it," Professor Christensen said. "Notice the statement at the beginning and the conclusion at the end; also notice the story: 'I invited people to play football, some showed up, I helped divide the teams, I suggested someone other than me be the star (quarterback) to best use resources, and people enjoyed playing football as a group because of my ability to plan and get people involved.'"

"Got it. Uhh, could you write that down so that I can use it?"

Professor Christensen laughed. "I wouldn't deprive you of the experience—plus, it'll be better if you tell the story."

Three Kinds of Scholarships

"While we are talking about stories," Professor Christensen continued, "let me tell you about the overall story that you must tell with your scholarship applications. There are, generally speaking, three kinds of scholarships: background-based scholarships, project-based scholarships, and merit-based scholarships. Every scholarship can be described as one, or a combination, of these three types.

"One: **Background-based scholarships** are for your heritage, your ethnicity, or what your progenitors have done. It may be that you come from a certain part of the country, went to a certain high school, or have ancestors in a specific ethnic category, or that someone semi-famous was a business partner or pioneer in an industry and left a scholarship legacy. These scholarships are based on your background and exclude individuals that don't fit the mold; you mostly need to be born into a circumstance, have a parent or step-parent, or be connected to someone who was a forerunner who did something to allow you to get this kind of a scholarship.

"Two: **Project-based scholarships** are based more on what you have done. Projects consist of writing essays, making a video, doing artwork, performing service, etc. This is where your scholarship is based on your effort, or a group effort, to complete something of value. This is like a 'show-and-tell' for scholarships, where you tell what you did.

"Three: **Merit-based scholarships** are determined by consistent effort leading to an accomplishment or accomplishments. Things like a high GPA, a musical competition, saving someone's life, raising livestock, or discovering a new process or product that benefits others are all examples. You will have had to have completed some accomplishment to merit the award. Most people cannot show up at a piano recital and expect to win; it takes years of practice to play a difficult piece of music extremely well. You must show that your life reflects the scholarship values and guidelines—that you deserve the scholarship."

Overarching Essay Story

"No matter what type of scholarship you apply for," Professor Christensen said, "you should allow your application to tell an overarching story. If you grew up in Maine and someone from your community offered a scholarship for descendants of lobster catchers, and your great-grandfather caught and sold lobsters—even for two years—then your essay needs to say that you have heard several of your great-grandfather's stories or tell about how you saw lobster catchers weekly during the summer. Paint a picture for the reader of your application, telling your overarching story, focusing on the type of scholarship, as you are copying and pasting your saved micro-essays."

"What are micro-essays?" Maria asked.

"Great question. I was about to explain," the professor said.

"Okay, sorry. I was just curious," Maria added sheepishly.

"No problem."

The professor continued, "What I want you to do is create micro-essays that are one to three paragraphs in length that show attributes of leadership, service, integrity, courage, overcoming hardships, and similar things. Write these micro-essays in a word processing program to check grammar and spelling, and then save the micro-essays in Excel or another spreadsheet program, with one essay in each cell. You may want to categorize these by topics such as leadership and service. When you are writing an essay, use these examples from your own life that you previously wrote and saved as micro-essays. All of you should have plenty of examples of service as you were required to offer one hour of service per week. Write these stories into segments. You can then copy and paste these segments into your essay to help you to write your paper faster."

Faster Source-Citing for Essays

"Big deal," Malcolm exclaimed, "even if I were to copy and paste, that still wouldn't speed me up that much."

"What do you mean? Have you ever tried using micro-essays?" Professor Christensen asked.

"Well, no. I can see your point, and it may speed me up some, but what I meant was, I can write fast enough, but I find myself spending more time trying to figure out how to cite my sources. One teacher wants it done in MLA, a scholarship wants it done in Chicago style, another organization wants it in APA; I spend hours just trying to meet their stupid requirements because I don't know what goes where," Malcolm responded with frustration.

"Interesting problem. What could you do to get out of your predicament?"

"I don't know…search the internet to find a grammar book?"

"Class, what is something Malcolm and anyone else could do, to help cite sources faster?"

There were several blank stares, but Tyler asked, "Why not use a citation generator?"

"What's that?" several people wanted to know.

"Well," Tyler began, "I needed to find out how to cite some sources for a paper and I did an internet search for 'MLA APA citation source' and I found something called a citation generator. There were several to choose from and so I played around with a few of them. I could pick the style and then enter a website, ISBN, or title and the generator filled in the rest. Now I don't have to worry about my format as the website does it for free."

"Would you recommend any particular one we can try out now?" Professor Christensen asked.

"Sure. I like citefast.com because it allows me to instantly create a bibliography in addition to the citations. I just punch in some basic information and it does the rest."

Professor Christensen brought it up in a browser projected onto the overhead screen. To try it out, he put in *Success Through a Positive Mental Attitude* and the site asked him to confirm the book.

"That's pretty handy," Professor Christensen said, "but I have an idea that could make this work better."

"What's that?" Tyler asked curiously.

"Go to ebay.com or amazon.com and enter your book title. This will allow you to use the ISBN and get the right edition, and then copy the ISBN into the Citefast generator. Let's try it." Professor Christensen went to eBay, entered the title, and chose one of the versions. Sure enough, in a matter of a few seconds, there was a perfectly cited source. He did it again, entering a page number. The citation came up perfectly.

"That is really useful, and will go perfectly with the assignment." Then addressing Malcolm, Professor Christensen said in a kind tone, "Did that help you to solve your problem?"

"I guess so."

"I just wanted to show you that simply complaining about a problem rarely solves it. Asking for solutions greatly enhances your capacity to accomplish your goals," Professor Christensen said. Malcolm scowled. "Class, I want you to use the remainder of the time to work on your micro-essays."

Justin, who was sitting next to Allison, wrote his two stories about visiting the nursing home and playing games with friends. He and Allison traded friendly jokes about how they would present their visit to the retirement center. He saved his essays for later use. As Justin finished saving his second essay and was submitting it to the class website, Professor Christensen dismissed the class.

What Can Happen with an Excess of Funds

Later that day, while at work, Justin checked his email and found that the campus tuition office had sent him an email.

Dear Mr. Murray,

You have overpaid your tuition. You need to tell us how you would like our office to process the excess funds. You can either apply the amount to next semester's tuition or take a check.

Sincerely,
Syracuse State University Tuition Office

Justin smiled. *I was able to keep the Pell Grant. I really did make over $800 an hour doing what was asked.* Justin replied, indicating that he'd like to have a check made available to him.

After submitting the reply to the tuition office, Justin took the lessons learned from his roommate and Professor Christensen and created some essays about his life experiences, saving the files for future reference. Justin realized: *I just created a system.*

Justin then decided to write a thank-you note to the scholarship committees telling them how much the scholarships meant to him. It felt good to express gratitude for how they made a difference.

Chapter 6: Principles and Suggestions

1. Decide now to apply to many different scholarships and grants during a semester. Aim for 20 to 50 applications.

2. Scholarships often will stack. The more you are awarded, the more money goes in your pocket. This doesn't work for every scholarship, but it can work for a large percentage of them.

3. Often you won't find out your hourly rate of pay until later. The rewards come as you are consistent in applying principles.

4. Find ways to show leadership and positive attributes in everyday activities.
   a. This idea works best if you can do this over time.
   b. Find everyday examples of attributes and use them.

5. There are three kinds of scholarships:
   a. **Background-Based Scholarship:** Your heritage, ethnicity, or religion, the part of the country you grew up in, or even hard things that have happened to you or your family determine your eligibility. You really didn't have to "do" anything in most cases to be able to claim these scholarships. You were most likely born into the required circumstances.
   b. **Project-Based Scholarship:** You do something to get something. This would be things like writing an essay, making a sculpture, taking a picture, participating in an activity such as a leadership summit, or giving service.
   c. **Merit-Based Scholarship:** This one requires a consistent amount of time and preparation to accomplish, and can be competitive. Examples are placing first in a piano competition, having a high GPA, winning a spelling bee, or raising a show animal. These take consistent work but can be the most rewarding.

6. There are three kinds of money seeds: 10% to tithing, 10% to savings (at least), and 10% to your dreams. While in college, one of your dreams should be to finish college debt-free.

7. Internships, scholarships, jobs, and classes have a timing component to them. If most people are applying to internships in the summer and going to school in the fall and winter, then you *may* find it helpful to be willing to go to school in the summer and work or do an internship in the summer. Check availability at different times of the year.

Chapter 6: Assignments

Get the free workbook at *www.FindingCollegeCash.com/FreeWB*

1. Enhance your essays.
    a. Use micro-essays and citefast.com to speed up the time it takes to create your essays. Use topic-relevant quotes.
    b. "Statement + Problem + Solution = Results as a Story."
    c. Save the essays as micro-essays that you can copy and paste.

2. Save all your essays for school assignments. You should back up your files to an online drive. With this idea, you can:
    a. Ask the teacher or a TA to review your paper and help you make it better.
    b. Get paid to write your essays by using them for scholarships.
    c. Save time for future essays.

3. Go be a leader by organizing a group to have fun or do service.
    a. Gather at least two other people to help you, but it can be tens or even hundreds of people.
    b. Tell this as a story you can use for scholarships.

4. Complete the "Money Seeds" and "Essay Ideas" exercises.

Chapter 6: Warnings and What to Avoid

1. Don't just literally copy and paste your essays. Take the time to review each essay and edit it as needed.

2. Please know that not every scholarship or financial aid resource can give you a check for any surplus. Some have rules against other forms of financial aid. However, you can decide which you will keep when you get them. Apply for every scholarship or resource that is available to you.

Chapter 7
Deciding What You Want

A few weeks later, Justin was doing homework at work, but what he was most excited to do was get some more free money. After having gone to the bank to deposit his paycheck and the check from the surplus of tuition funds, Justin now had thousands of dollars in his account. While he had to wait in line for about ten minutes, he was excited to cash his checks. Seeing firsthand that scholarships really are free money, he wanted some more.

At this point, Justin had applied for seven scholarships and won two. Even though he hadn't won five of the scholarships, he had ample proof that applying for them paid off. He had spent about twenty-four hours on the seven applications and essays and had gotten thousands of dollars. Taking the total amount of money he had received from the Pell Grant, the Osborn scholarship, and the $120 from his dad's employer, he was getting paid hundreds of dollars per hour. *I can't think of a higher paying job; even if I had only gotten the Pell Grant, it would have been worth it.*

What most excited him was that now, thanks to the advice from his roommate and teacher, he had a system. Justin spent the rest of his time at work applying to scholarships through Fastweb. He wanted to refine his system and see how it worked, so he chose to try it out on scholarships for under $1,000 each, saving the more lucrative scholarships for when he had more time for applications and revisions. He was able to apply to two of these "smaller" scholarships with this new system before leaving work. *It used to take me a few days to do this, but now I can do it in a few hours.*

On Wednesday, Allison and Justin, who were oh-so incidentally sitting in adjacent seats, smiled at each other. Professor Christensen began in an engaging voice, "I hope that you are beginning to see the power of applying for financial aid and scholarships. Some students earn more than what college costs. Others earn millions of dollars in scholarships. Others will take some of their excess money and purchase a house while in college that they rent out. That is a big goal, but completely possible. However, to accomplish this you will need to continue to apply to scholarships. We will discuss this in-depth later on in the semester.[18] To even begin doing something that big, you must first learn to master your money."

Getting What You Really Want

Justin rolled his eyes a little. *Here it comes. He's going to tell us to scrimp and save some more.*

"At the end of this assignment, I'm going to ask you to pick a really big goal to spend your money on, and we're going to create a plan to get there," the Professor said.

Huh? thought Justin. *Why is he telling us to spend money? Don't all finance guys tell you to scrimp?*

"In fact," Professor Christensen said, "I want to ask everyone here: What's something really fun that you would like to do? Things like going on a cruise, buying a new electronic gizmo, going on a road trip, getting a ski pass, having a fantastic wedding—what do you *really* want to do, assuming that it was possible? Shout out your answers," the Professor Christensen encouraged.

"I want to go on a road trip to San Diego."

"Go to Six Flags."

"I want to buy a new laptop."

"I want to go on a study-abroad to Europe."

"I'd like to buy a new outfit."

"I want to buy a new tablet."

---

18 See Finding College Cash: Housing by the author.

"I want to buy a bullet bike."

Justin thought for a moment. *What* do *I really want to do?* He decided and spoke up. "I want to go to Chichen Itza." He had wanted to go since he was in Mexico, but saying it aloud in front of others made him feel weird.

A few other replies came, including a wedding, flight instruction to get a pilot's license, and a backpacking trip.

"Good," said Professor Christensen. "I want to help you all achieve your dreams. Let me share two quotes with you and then tell you a story. Will Rogers said, 'Too many people spend money they haven't earned, to buy things they don't want, to impress people they don't like.'[19]

"I'd be willing to guess that everyone here could, in less than one hour and with the aid of the internet, spend a million dollars, if it were given to them, and if they had the desire to spend it. College makes it incredibly easy to spend money on useless junk that doesn't matter. There is *never* an income high enough that you can't outspend it. As a Japanese proverb says: 'Getting money is like digging with a needle; spending it is like water soaking into sand.'[20] It is incredibly easy to spend money on worthless junk; I am asking you to spend your money on what matters to you and give up the insignificant things.

You Can Always Outspend Your Income

"My mother-in-law and father-in-law went to college earning a student wage, which isn't much at all. They did just fine living on that small amount, having a food budget of just a few dollars a week! They never went into debt. Well, my father-in-law got a job after graduation and suddenly started making five times their combined student wages, and they were blown away. My parents-in-law exclaimed, 'Wow! How are we ever going to spend this much?' But it

---

19 Goodreads. "Quote by Will Rogers: "Too many people spend money they haven't earned...."Accessed August 9, 2017. www.goodreads.com/quotes/42553-too-many-people-spend-money-they-haven-t-earned-to-buy.

20 Quoteland.com. "Money Quotes." Accessed August 9, 2017. www.quoteland.com/topic/Money-Quotes/101/.

didn't take long. Suddenly, they started asking themselves by the end of the month, 'Where did our money go?' They decided to write down every purchase they made to find out where they were spending their money. To their great surprise, they found that their money was disappearing due to a bunch of little nickel-and-dime types of things that they were buying—fifty cents here, two dollars there, twenty-five cents there.

"Obviously, fifty cents back then was worth more than it is now, but the point is that my parents-in-law stopped being aware of their spending. The money disappeared because they didn't control their spending habits. They were not spending *on purpose*. Fortunately, my father-in-law made corrections that we'll talk about in a moment.[21] Now I am NOT going to tell you to write down every penny, but I will show you a system so that you won't need to worry about your money.

"If you are spending your money on useless items, it's time to become *aware* of how you're spending your money. You don't have to eliminate *all* useless spending, just most of it. What do I mean by useless items and useless spending? A small bag of chips that costs four dollars at a snack shop; eating fast food every day; letting food go to waste; going to new releases of multiple movies per year; buying new gaming consoles or games, and so on. Spending your money on things that you don't truly value, or that offer fleeting satisfaction, is called your *bubblegum-diamond-thief.*™

"What's that?" A girl asked.

"A *bubblegum-diamond-thief* is what costs you money. To illustrate, let me ask you: how long does bubblegum last?"

"Maybe an hour," she said with a shrug.

"How long would your mother keep her wedding ring diamond?"

"Forever; she'd never let it go."

"Why the difference in time for those two items?"

"The diamond has value and reminds her of how much she loves my dad, while the bubblegum is worthless after it has been used."

---

21 This is a true story about the author's real father- and mother-in-law.

"That is exactly the point. If you buy too many bubblegum-type items—things that offer only temporary satisfaction—you lose out on your diamond-type items—the things that you really want and that really matter to you. Choose things that build memories.

Common Bubblegum-Diamond-Thieves—Avoid Debt

"Let me give you an analogy. Has anyone here ever used a coupon?" Several class members nodded. "Can you imagine going to the checkout register and handing the clerk a coupon that said 'pay an additional 15%'? The clerk gives you a 15% discount, but you correct the clerk and say 'No, no, no, this coupon was to cost me 15% more—so 115% of the purchase price. Please change my order; I wanted to pay 15% more.' Can you imagine the confused look on the clerk's face?"

"Why would anyone actually do that?" Justin asked.

Professor Christensen smiled. "I agree!" He said with emphasis, "Why *would* anyone hand the clerk a coupon to pay more? But people do it every day when they pay with credit cards and don't pay them off—only instead of 15%, they pay up to 29% and then carry a balance they have to keep paying year after year. Instead of buying something else, people waste money paying interest."

Justin got the point: *Interest is an expensive waste of cash.*

"What are some other ways college students waste money?" Professor Christensen asked the class.

"Alcohol and cigarettes."

"Fast food."

"Gasoline."

"Clothes and makeup," a guy said.

"*Video games and cars,*" a girl retorted.

"Okay," interjected Professor Christensen. "Let's keep it friendly. You can easily see the point: Money can disappear in an instant, but take a long time to regain. I'm glad you mentioned cars. Having a car, even if it is fully paid off, costs about $300 per month to own. The approximate average monthly costs are $100 for gasoline, $100 for insurance, and $100 for licensing, maintenance, repairs, and registration.[22] When you only make $1,000 to $2,000 per month before taxes, $300 is a lot of money. Even if I was wrong and it is $200 per month, that is $200 times 48 months of college equals $9,600 over a four-year time frame. Let's say I am wrong again and you get a car with a car or lease payment (by the way, leasing a car is one of the most expensive ways to have a car—only importing a car or buying a high-end luxury car is more expensive). In addition to the approximate $300 per month to operate the car, you have a $499 payment. This would be $799 per month times 48 months equals $38,352 AND you still would owe about $6,000 on the car when you finish college (due to a decline in value or finishing the lease). For most students, having a car in college almost forces them to have debt.

"You may think you should have a car to get a higher-paying job that is farther from campus. However, after subtracting the approximate $300 extra cost, you have to ask yourself if the job is actually paying you more. If you can get a job for $8 an hour on campus and a job that pays $10 an hour twenty minutes from campus, you should pick the $8-per-hour job as it will save you time and money. Cars are *bubblegum-diamond-thieves* that are really sneaky because you feel that it is a justifiable expense, but it actually costs you money. You need to ask yourself: 'Am I willing to spend $300 a month or more to own a car?' If not, sell it and buy a bicycle or student bus pass. Another option is to use Uber or Lyft through free apps you can download on your smartphone; you only pay when you use the service, and can get picked up from most locations.

"I want to teach you proactive strategies to earn money and defensive strategies to keep money. You need both to win at money.

Spending on Purpose

"This is why I recommend that you pick something fun, something that you really want. You have the ability to *choose* how you spend your money.

---

22 Based on observations of the author, not a study

Get your friends involved in this. Plan a really big event, such as going to Europe, going on a road trip, or something else you want. Tell your friends, 'In eight months, let's go do _____ (whatever your goal is) together. And let's start saving now.' You'll find that people are usually 'on board' to do something fun or adventurous, and planning in advance adds to the adventure and possibilities.

"This also becomes your beacon at the moment of decision. You can decide how to spend your money. When you're shopping or when friends want to go out and splurge, remind yourself that you're saving up to do your fun activity—your *Diamond*. Tell your friends something like, 'I'm saving up for a road trip (or whatever). Could we *rent* a movie, instead of going to the theater?' Simply purchasing your food from the store—and saving dining out for important planned events—really helps to save money. So, class, I want to teach you how to spend your money the *smart* way, on purpose.

Offense + Defense + Strategy = Success

"Class, throughout this semester, I am going to share with you fast ways to make and keep your money. You will need to have offensive and defensive strategies.

"Do I have anyone here who likes sports?" Several people nodded or raised their hands. "Can anyone tell me which sport you will win if you use only defense?" No answer came.

"All right, how about if your strategy is strictly offense—would you win?"

"If you can score more points than the other team," a girl ventured.

"Okay," the professor stated, "what sport do you play?"

"Basketball."

"If your team were to try to score with the other team defending, it would take you around 20 seconds per shot to make a basket—if not more. But if you were to not have any players at the opposing basket to defend, the other team would be able to make a shot in probably ten seconds if they staggered their players. Even if they missed, because your team is playing strictly offense, they would be the only team going after the ball, and their team would get the rebound. Just on time, they would be more likely to win because it took them only 10–20 seconds to make a shot, whereas it took you 20–35 seconds to score. The other team would win even if your players were more skilled offensively; the only exception would be if their defense was so bad that it wasn't even a challenge, but even then you would have to score faster than they did to win."

"But if I use offense and defense, I'm still not guaranteed to win," the girl retorted.

"True, but your odds of success go up drastically using both," Professor Christensen replied. "If you use both principles, it then comes down to strategy and skill, along with consistent effort. Even if your skills were *unstoppable*, your strategy could sink your game; on the other hand, if you had a great strategy but no skills, you would lose. You need to strategize using offense and defense and increase your skills. Lastly, if you did nothing to implement or practice both, you would be out of shape."

The girl nodded in agreement.

Assignment for Offense and Defense

Professor Christensen again addressed the class. "Within the past few weeks, you were given the assignment to apply to FAFSA and at least six scholarships. As an offensive strategy, I am going to assign that everyone here apply for 30 scholarships. You only need 24 more to complete the assignment; whether you want to do them all at once or over the semester, it doesn't matter to me, but they need to be done and submitted to the class website. This is an offensive strategy. Let's take a vote. Would you rather have me give you an offensive or defensive strategy that you can immediately use?"

"If by offense you mean making more money, let's do that one first," Tyler said. "I could use the extra cash."

Other students readily agreed. Professor Christensen smiled and said, "I knew that you would pick that one. It almost always is chosen first. It's a lot more interesting to make money—or at least that is what people think. Before I tell you the strategy, I want you to remember: *It is what you keep— not make, that matters*. Nonetheless, I'll teach you all a proactive money tip.

An Idea to Get Your Employer to Pay for Tuition

"Go to your employer's human resources department and ask if there is tuition assistance, a tuition reimbursement program, or an employee scholarship program; ask what is required to participate and see if you are eligible. Most employers will require that you stay with the company for at least a year; however, if you ever are required to pay all or part back, there is usually an interest-free repayment plan. This is far better than a student loan because you don't have to pay interest. However, if you get to keep the money—especially as a scholarship—this is a great resource.

"If your employer does not presently offer a scholarship or a tuition reimbursement program, tell your employer this: 'I have found a way to reduce the company's taxes that will save the company from having to pay thousands of dollars.' Your employer, or boss, will be interested at the thought of tax savings. Then say, 'One of the tax exemptions allowed by the IRS is that employers can deduct educational expenses up to $5,250, per employee, each year by offering help with tuition. If I were to go to the company accountant and verify how much the company would save, would you be willing to save money on taxes by helping to pay for my tuition expenses?' Keep in mind that your employer may add other conditions, but just by asking you may be able to save yourself money. Just so you know, tuition aids above $5,250 will be taxed as part of your wages. Now one important tip is this: Whether or not you are getting tuition reimbursement from your employer, be the best employee that you can. You never know if at the end of the year, or another time, your boss will decide to offer this to you. Show you are a good employee and worth the investment."

"But that seems like so much work," Maria complained. "Besides, I'd be so nervous to talk to my boss."

"Ok," said Professor Christensen, "which requires more work, spending maybe an hour getting tuition reimbursement of up to $5,250 (or more), working about 600 hours at $10 per hour to get the $5,250 after taxes, or spending 10–20 years paying back student loans? Any one of those three methods can help you pay for tuition, but it only would take about 10 minutes to ask and 45 minutes to fill out any paperwork to get the tuition reimbursement."

"Well, if you put it that way." Maria said, "I guess it would be easier to at least see if I could get tuition reimbursement—but I am still afraid to talk to my boss."

"Class, what could someone who is scared to talk to a boss do to help himself or herself ask about tuition reimbursement?"

"Practice on a friend."

"Schedule an appointment to talk."

"Bring in your recent positive employee evaluation to add credibility."

"Send an email to HR."

"Email your boss."

"Great ideas," said the professor. "Those ideas can help each of you talk with your boss. Let's move on to defensive strategies."

529 Savings Plans—A Fast Way to Save Big

"I'd like to change topics," Professor Christensen began. "What if I offered you a coupon that would give you up to a 15% (but more likely 2 to 6%) discount on your tuition? Would you use it?"

"I'd sure jump on that," Malcolm said. "But what school is going to offer any discount on tuition?"

"Has anyone heard of a 529 Education Savings Plan?" the professor asked.

A few people kind of shrugged.

"For example, the Utah Education Savings Plan (UESP)[23] offers a five percent state income tax credit. If you were to open an account, put your tuition money in, then take it out, you could use it for a college or trade school and get a five percent credit on your state taxes. This means that if you were to open a 529 UESP, you could get an instant discount on your taxes (or the taxes of your parents or guardian, whoever owned the account) for contributing to your 529 Savings Plan. As a bonus, any money grows tax-free on all interest and gains, so you won't get taxed as long as the money is used for qualified expenses—so if your money grows 10–40% you won't be taxed on the gains."

"What are qualified expenses?" Allison asked.

"Tuition, lab or class fees, books, and housing," Professor Christensen replied. "If expenses are for non-qualified purchases, you will be taxed and penalized on the gains. Here are some things you should know."

List of Questions to Ask Representatives of 529 ESP

- Where does the plan allow the beneficiary to use the money (what types of institutions)?
- What do I need to do to get the money out and have it count as a qualified expense? Does it come by check or electronically?
- Will I be reimbursed, will the money go to my school, or will I need to get a special debit card or checkbook to get my money?
- Who is the guardian or custodian of the money, and are there rules for taking withdrawals?
- Are there any state tax credits for investing in a 529 ESP in your state (or the state in which you are going to school)?
- What are the fees associated with the 529 savings plan I choose? (The fees vary among plans.)
- What investment funds are available in the plan?
- (Optional) For those who are under the state poverty level, is

---

23 Compare with the plan in your state.

there any type of match offered for contributions, in addition to the gains earned?

"Here is a handout that compares the benefits of the various 529 savings plans among states. [See Assignments.] You can easily save 32% or more by saving for college rather than borrowing money with student loans.

"Just by opening a 529 ESP and paying your tuition, books, and rent with a 529 savings plan, you can potentially get a 5% discount by not having to pay Utah state income tax. Also, you can save by not having to pay tax on your gains. If you go to a different school in another state, there are different, but similar, resources available."

"You mean that we can get a 5% discount on tuition, books, and rent just for putting money in, then immediately pay for school from a 529 Education Savings Plan?" Maria asked.

"It will depend on how much you pay in income tax, but the short answer is pretty much, yes—if your 529 savings plan allows it." Professor Christensen replied. "The tax credit goes to the account owner when tax returns are filed, but this is a great opportunity to get a tax credit—which acts as a gain, in preventing a loss. It works out as a great strategy. Some states don't have an income tax credit offer, but like all 529 savings plans, they still offer tax-free gains for qualified expenses."

"I am so doing that," Maria said.

"Keep in mind the limits of what school costs because, unless it is a qualified expense, you will be penalized. This is just another game that the IRS requires that we play," Professor Christensen said. "This is all part of the complexity of the present tax code. It does require jumping through some hoops, but the rewards are worth it.

Routes to Wealth and Paying for School

"There are *slow* ways to wealth, medium ways, faster ways, plain *dumb luck*, and dishonest methods to earn money. Let's talk about all of them.

"First, the sheer luck and dishonest methods: win the lottery, inherit money, win a sweepstakes, win a tournament, cheat, lie, steal, defraud others, run a scam, and take credit for someone else's work. These methods are mostly determined by chance (specific non-repeatable situations) and poor ambition. While they can happen, they are not repeatable for everyone. Just because you know someone who did something dishonest and got away with it, it doesn't mean that you will get the same results. Just because you see someone win the lottery, it doesn't mean you'll be able to win. These events happen by chance; they are almost impossible to replicate and are really a waste of time, effort, energy, and money.

"You won't find many millionaires playing the lottery. True, there are some who play, but on the whole, millionaires realize it's a game of chance and a waste of time and money. Irrespective of who you are, for each lottery ticket that you buy, your chances of picking six correct numbers between one and ninety-nine are fewer than one out of 1,120,529,256—even worse if sequence matters. Roger Jones said, 'I think of lotteries as a tax on the mathematically challenged.'[24] Most of the people who play the lottery are the poorer class of people,[25] as they expect to 'hit it big.'[26] They dream of easy wealth but are unwilling to do what most of you did today—that is, take action toward their goals.

"For those who win the lottery, their lives change drastically, as winners are often threatened, sued, and sometimes killed.[27] Even if those negative events don't happen, there is a greater sense of satisfaction in earning the money *yourself*—the 'I built this!' 'I accomplished this!' and 'I overcame this!' attitudes

---

24 Jones, Roger. "Quotes About Lottery." Good Reads. Accessed August 9, 2017. http://www.goodreads.com/quotes/tag/lottery.

25 Clotfelter, Charles T. "Do Lotteries Hurt the Poor? Well, Yes and No." Duke Policy News. Accessed August 9, 2017. http://news2.sanford.duke.edu/newsletters/dpn/summer00/lottery.html.

26 Hopkins, Christopher A. "Personal finance: Lottery mania hurts low-income players." Times Free Press. Accessed August 9, 2017. http://www.timesfreepress.com/news/2012/dec/05/1205c-personal-finance-lottery-mania-hurts-low/.

27 'Hannah'. "How the Lives of 10 Lottery Millionaires went Disastrously Wrong." money.co.uk. Accessed August 9, 2017. http://www.money.co.uk/article/1002156-how-the-lives-of-10-lottery-millionaires-went-disasterously-wrong.htm#ixzz2LlGOA2mb.

you get from following principles that require you to think, work, and grow. Lotteries, inheritances, tournaments, contests, or other lucky wins deprive you of that satisfaction, and since you didn't earn it, you don't value it as much. Incidentally, most lottery winners are back to where they were financially within five years of winning. My goal is to help you all gain financial independence. Since we cannot replicate with accuracy the *lucky* approach, we are eliminating it from this class, and I suggest eliminating it from your lives because it is a waste of time and money."

Tyler interjected, "Excuse me professor, but why did you mention contests as being bad? I see lots of no-essay-required scholarships that just require me to enter my name and email address. Wouldn't it be beneficial for me to enter 100 contests?"

How to Spot a Scam Scholarship or Time Waster

Turning to Tyler, Professor Christensen said, "I am so glad you asked that question. Let me answer that by asking you a question. If it was easy to get money for college that way, how many people do you think would apply to that contest?"

"I don't know," Tyler said. "Maybe 10,000 people."

"We'll go with that number," the professor said. "First, why do you think that they make it so easy? I'll tell you. They are collecting the names and email addresses and then selling them to companies and organizations to spam you. Applying to many of those contests will fill your email with junk. Because those companies have, based on what you said, 10,000 or maybe 100,000 people applying every three months, they make the money back with a profit. While they may give out some money, there are very low odds of you winning. Furthermore, there may not be any way to verify that someone actually won. It could just be a made-up name and stock photo.

"Now, I am not saying that all contests are bad, just that you should be careful about what you apply for. Any legitimate scholarship should have an email, address, or other contact method for questions. Legitimate scholarships will fit into one of the three kinds of scholarships we talked about earlier: background-based, project-based, or merit-based. Legitimate scholarships generally will *NOT* ask for your social security number. And generally, legitimate scholarships will apply to only a select group of people.

"If you still want to apply to contests that only require your name, email, and contact info, I would suggest that you limit your time to say one or two hours per month, and use a separate email account for handling spam—because you may not want to have it go to your primary email.

"That being said about contests," the professor continued, "don't confuse them with competitions. Competitions can be very profitable when you are seeking money for college—even if they call it a contest. Competitions can offer cash, prizes, and more. The main difference is that they require you to complete a project. There are competitions for college students that offer what are called 'cash awards.' These competitions might involve business, public speaking, engineering, math-a-thon, decathlon, fitness, skill testing, etc. These are some great venues for gaining cash for college. You definitely would like to include these as part of your strategy for paying for college. Even if you don't win, you can list 'participant,' 'finalist,' etc. on your résumé as you would 'scholarship.' Additionally, these competitions have few competitors. **Prepare** by being the best you can at your skill, **find** competitions that you enjoy, **apply** for the competition, **receive** critiques by judges, and **build** from what you learn and gain."

Professor Christensen said, "After that long-winded explanation of some things to *avoid*, let me tell you a defensive strategy. This is something anyone can use regardless of background or GPA.

Start of Defensive Strategies

"For defense," Professor Christensen continued, "every person should read or listen to a book called *Out of Debt, to Prosperity*.[28] I cannot begin to tell you how ridiculously people behave, including many of our local, state, and

---

28 This book will be available by the author.

federal governments, spending more money than they bring in. And they have to work harder to pay off the interest. I hope that you really take to heart this lesson on getting what you really want and managing your money.

"As an additional strategy, I want you to pick one to three goals that are meaningful to you. You need to make a realistic plan to save up for that goal. For example, save X dollars per month, take a second job, start a business, eliminate a specific activity that you don't really value—saving you Y dollars per period, or something similar. We are going to then use these goals in our next class."

"Whoa," said Malcolm. "With the X's and Y's, you'd think we were in a math class."

Professor Christensen chuckled along with several class members. "To be fair, you do get math credit for taking the class, but don't worry—nothing too hard to grasp."

You Can Make It

A few hours later, Justin's chat window sounded. *Pling*. It was his dad.

"Hey Justin, how are you?"

"Good," Justin replied. "College has been fun."

"Do you need anything? I feel really bad that I can't pay for your college like I said I would. Are you doing all right?"

"Dad, I am in a class that is teaching me how to apply for scholarships, manage money, etc. Don't worry, I'll be fine."

Justin was more and more sure of that statement as he thought about what Professor Christensen had taught him, and now that he had more money because of the Pell Grant, he was excited.

"Dad, don't worry. I have already paid for tuition, books, and my rent for this month. I forgot to tell you and Mom, but I was awarded a scholarship for incoming freshmen, plus I was given a Pell Grant—I can keep the extra money. With my job, I'll be fine."

"Well, a fine time to tell your family! That's great news!"

"Sorry, I've been busy. And, yes, it is good news for me."

"Well, congratulations. Don't worry about it. I'm glad to hear that you're doing well. Keep your mom and me posted."

"I will," Justin said as he and his dad continued chatting. His dad had taken a second job to help make ends meet. Justin was grateful for Professor Christensen's assignment to apply early for scholarships. It had saved his bacon. He decided that he was going to apply for as many scholarships as he could this semester. He logged into Fastweb and started looking for other scholarships.

Chapter 7: Principles and Suggestions

1. Deciding on something fun to do can help you save your money. What do you want to do?

2. Decide now to apply to many different scholarships and grants during a semester. I recommend 30 to 50 applications.

3. Go to www.FindingCollegeCash.com, where you can learn about both offensive and defensive money strategies.

4. *Bubblegum-diamond-thieves* steal your money. They include buying too many things that you don't value and wasting your money on things like interest, expensive items, and impulse buys.

5. Employers can be a good resource for paying for school.

6. Scholarships generally stack. The more you are awarded, the more money goes in your pocket.

7. You may be able to get a state income tax credit by using a 529 Education Savings, and not be taxed on your gains if you use the money for tuition, books, housing (up to the dorm limits), class fees, and lab fees.

Chapter 7: Assignments

1. Complete "A Word on Goals" in the workbook. Pick a really big goal and make a viable plan to get what you really want (e.g., save X dollars

per month, take a second job, start a business, eliminate a specific activity that you don't really value, saving you Y dollars per period, or something similar).

2. Complete the "Ask Your Employer to Pay Tuition" to see if there are any tuition, book, housing, or other perks of your job. Contact the human resources department or your boss directly.

3. (Encouraged) Sell your car. It costs an approximate average of $300 per month to own a car. Even if this was $200 per month, that is $9,600 over four years. If you have an additional $499/month car payment, this number goes to $38,352.
    a. Buy a bus pass
    b. Get a bicycle
    c. Walk
    d. Get a job on or near campus
    e. Get rides with friends (offer to pay for part of the ride)
    f. Use services like Uber or Lyft

4. Complete the "529 Education Savings Plans" exercise.

Chapter 7: Warnings and What to Avoid

1. Be sincere with your boss about needing money for college.

2. Don't try to do exclusively offense or defense; both are needed for financial success.

3. Avoid waiting until the last minute. The earlier you can apply for scholarships, the more you can earn.

4. If you use the money from a 529 Education Savings Plans on something that is not deemed a qualified expense, you will be taxed on the money taken out and assessed a penalty.

Chapter 8
Money Mastery

Justin applied for three scholarships over the next two days; two of them were for under $1,000, so the application was not as in-depth. For the third, Justin wanted to use an essay he had written for a class; it turned out that he could use parts of the essay, but needed to modify it. Following his roommate Nate's advice, this time when he applied, he copied and pasted the commonly asked questions, like his first name, last name, major, high school GPA, class standing, address, etc. Justin also created some micro-essays. He was able to submit the two smaller scholarship applications in less than three hours. Justin submitted screenshots to the class website.

Justin saved his information so that the next time he applied for a scholarship, it would only be a matter of copying and pasting to the appropriate fields. It was really easy. While Justin had only been awarded a few scholarships at this point, he was still willing to apply so that he would have the option of getting money. *It's like Mr. Wheatley's example about flying standby: If I apply, I <u>might</u> get a scholarship, but if I don't at least apply, I won't.*

Justin's Goals—Finding Your Motivation

Justin wanted to take Professor Christensen's assignment regarding his goals seriously. He submitted the following:

1. Go to Chichen Itza for spring break my sophomore year.
2. Graduate without student loans or credit card debt.
3. Have money saved up to buy a property.

Justin's first goal was his motivating goal. He was excited because he had wanted to go to Chichen Itza ever since being in Mexico; it had become a dream. The other goals were indefinite, as he didn't know the exact timing or how he would achieve them. Justin decided for his basic plan that he was going to save $30 every two weeks from his paycheck. Also, he was going to pay half of whatever unexpected money came his way from things like birthdays and Christmas toward his goals.

You Don't Have to Spend Much to Have Fun

Justin really wanted to take Allison out on a date. He just didn't know how to make the transition. It was one thing to have her as a study-buddy and homework helper, but it was a completely different matter to ask her out. Justin thought, *Well, I guess the best thing to do is to just ask her.* So, he came up with several ideas—going to a park to Frisbee, playing tennis (he could offer to teach her if she didn't know how to play), or finding a local hike to go on. Afterward, they could go to dinner.

Justin asked his roommates about a good, but inexpensive place to eat. "Why not invite her here for dinner or go on a picnic together?" one of his roommates suggested. "At least that way, if things go south, you haven't shelled out a lot of cash for a first date. I mean, you can always take her out to eat later when your relationship develops."

"That's a really good idea," Justin said. He thanked his roommates and started making plans. He didn't know how Allison would feel about being invited to his place on the first date, so he decided on a picnic at the park. Justin planned a menu and realized just how valuable his roommate's advice was. Justin didn't even know if Allison was dating someone else, or if she was interested in going out with him. At least by planning a picnic, he wasn't out twenty to forty dollars.

Justin and Allison had exchanged phone numbers at one study group and he had put her number in his phone contacts. Grabbing the bull by the horns, he gave her a call.

"Hello, Allison. This is Justin from cl—"

"Hi, Justin! How are you?" Allison answered.

"I'm doing all right. Hey, I was wondering if you'd like to go to a park to play tennis or go biking and then have a picnic with me this Saturday."

She said, "Yeah! That sounds great! What did you have in mind?"

"I'd like to go play tennis, but if you don't know how to play, we can play Frisbee or go biking."

"That sounds fun. Let's play tennis. I once had a roommate who taught me a little."

"Sounds good. I have two rackets and some tennis balls. I can come to your place or meet you on campus. Which do you prefer?"

"We always seem to be on campus. Let's go to the park."

Justin said, "All right. I'll come by and pick you up at three o'clock on Saturday? Will that work?"

"Sounds good to me. If the park isn't too far, could we walk?"

"Yeah, I think that will work."

"Great," Allison said, "I'll see you then." They ended the call pleasantly.

Yes! Justin couldn't help thinking after he hung up the phone.

Saturday came and Justin was surprised at how nervous he was, especially since he had already spent so much time with her. But this was different; this was a date. Justin arrived at Allison's apartment a little early, did a breath and B.O. check and went to the door. Allison opened it to his knock.

Justin smiled and was about to comment on her T-shirt and basketball shorts, but before he could say anything, she said: "Hey, Justin, you look really nice today!"

"Thanks," he said. "I was about to say the same to you."

"Thanks," Allison said with a smile.

"So, are you ready to play?"

"Yeah!"

Justin and Allison walked to the park and found the tennis court. "You said that your roommate taught you a little bit of how to play. Would you like to start a game or practice a little first?"

"Why don't we just start a game?" Allison said.

They started to play and Justin was impressed. Her swing was pretty good! You could tell that she was a novice tennis player, but she did well.

"Hey, you're pretty good."

"Yeah, I used to play softball in high school," Allison said. "I guess it kind of carries over."

"You are full of surprises!"

Justin let Allison win a game, but he won twice. Both had fun. Allison and Justin went to a nearby grassy field and started getting the food out.

"I hope you like Mexican food, 'cuz that's what we're having."

"Smells good."

"They're tortas—kind of a grilled, open-face sandwich."

When the food was ready, they sat down and started talking. Justin found out that Allison's dad was a barber and that she was paying her own way through college.

Justin described his family and some of the events that had happened in his life, including the humanitarian service that he had done a few years ago, and she talked about having always wanted to study abroad. The rest of the evening went fairly well. After their dinner, Justin walked Allison to her apartment and went home.

Parable of Instant Returns

At class the next week Professor Christensen had everyone sit in a semicircle around him. He then asked, "Who wants to trade ten dollars to receive twenty dollars?" Everyone raised a hand.

Professor Christensen repeated, "Who wants to trade ten dollars to receive twenty dollars?" Again, everyone raised his or her hand or made comments of acceptance.

For a third time, the professor asked, "Who wants to trade ten dollars to receive twenty dollars?"

Most students raised their hands, but Tyler got up pulled out his wallet and removed a ten-dollar bill. He walked over to Professor Christensen, handed him the ten-dollar bill, and said, "I do." Professor Christensen pulled out a crisp twenty-dollar bill and handed it to Tyler. Professor Christensen then asked the class:

"Excluding those who already participated, who wants to trade five dollars to receive ten dollars?"

The students now understood what game Professor Christensen was playing. This time, students began jumping up for their wallets and purses. It was a race among students, and Allison got there first.

"Here's five dollars," Allison said. Professor Christensen handed her the ten-dollar bill and received the five-dollar bill. Professor Christensen began again:

"Excluding those who've already participated, who wants to trade two dollars to receive five dollars?"

Justin didn't have his wallet, and he didn't have any cash on him, so he watched as five dollars were exchanged for two dollars. When it hit one dollar for two dollars, one student tried to write an I.O.U. note, but Professor Christensen said he only accepted cash.

"Either you have it, or you don't," the professor said.

The student returned to his seat in the semi-circle. One dollar was traded for two dollars, and the one-dollar bill went into Professor Christensen's pocket. Students started griping that they didn't have their money with them.

"Let's keep a positive attitude," Professor Christensen said in a cheerful tone.

"How did it feel to watch others getting a deal while you didn't, knowing that if you had had the available cash, you would have gladly made the same deal for yourself?" the professor asked the class.

"Jealous."

"Eager."

"Anticipating how I could get cash."

"Upset!"

The students answered nearly all at once.

"I want you all to learn some very big lessons from this example," Professor Christensen said. "First, money talks, words walk. In other words, you can only take advantage of opportunities if you have the cash available—it may not be *your* cash, but you do need to have it available. Second, it *is* possible to make an instant return on your money. Third, I needed to get a dollar for a toll road, and the attendant never has the right change," the professor added with a smile. The students laughed.

"How can we apply these lessons?" Professor Christensen asked.

"Always carry cash," Tyler said.

"Well, I would recommend that you decide on how much is right for you," Professor Christensen replied. "But for students, carrying about ten dollars on your person may be a good idea. Consider carrying a pre-paid debit or special debit card that works like cash. It's more secure than cash, but allows you to keep within predefined limits. What else did you learn from this example?"

Justin raised his hand and said, "It was more than just having the cash; it was also taking action with that cash. When you first asked us about trading the $10 for $20, all of us raised our hands, but only the one who was willing to get out of his seat and take action received any money."

"Good," said the professor. "We're taught to raise our hands, and while that is movement, it is not an action that leads you to the goal. Excellent! What else can we learn?"

Allison responded. "We can learn from watching others and then take similar actions. When Tyler got up and exchanged his ten dollars for twenty, we all watched. I figured something similar might happen again, so I pulled out my wallet."

"Great!" the professor said. "We can learn both things to *do* and things to *avoid* by watching others. Whom you watch also matters: if you learn from a garbage man, you can learn how to gather garbage. If you learn from a millionaire, you can learn how to be a millionaire. Brian Tracy said, 'Model the best people in your industry. Imitate what the best do.'[29] If we can learn to do what people who manage their money well do, then we will benefit. Any other lessons learned from the example?"

Maria raised her hand. "I have a question. You said a moment ago that it's possible to get an instant return on your money. Could you explain how to do that?"

401(k) Plans and Benefits of Starting Early

"This is a slower method, but it's literally the same thing as our example of exchanging money at the beginning of class today. If your employer matches 25%, then for every $10 you put in, you get $12.50, total—your $10 plus $2.50—up to whatever limit is set by your employer. With a one-to-one match, for every $10 you put in, you get another $10. Keep in mind that for any 401(k) plan, your employer will probably request that you stay for at least a year, but if you ever quit or change jobs, you can take all that money with you and put it in your new job's 401(k) plan or you can roll it over to an IRA or Roth IRA.

The advantage is that your money is working for you. The stock market has averaged about 10% annual return over a 15-to-20-year period.[30] The earlier you start a 401(k), the more time your money has to grow. And not only does *your* money grow, but your employer's *match* also grows.

"Let me show you how much your money can grow in 40 years. If you were to put in $100 each month, and that was matched by your employer with another $60 (a 60% contribution match—60% being a semi-average match rate) for a total of $160 per month, and then just did this until

---

29 See Tracy, Brian. *Flight Plan How to Achieve More, Faster Than You Ever Dreamed Possible.* San Francisco, Calif: Berrett-Koehler Publishers, 2008.

30 Anspach, Dana. "Historical Stock Market Returns—Stock Market Returns Since 1973." About.com Money Over 55. Accessed August 9, 2017. http://moneyover55.about.com/od/howtoinvest/a/marketreturns.htm

retirement at each job you have for 40 years, averaging a 10% return, then you would have over $1.02 million and would have put in a total of $48,000 of your personal money. If you had wanted to reach $1 million in only ten years instead of 40, then you would have had to have put in $279 each month, again matched at a 60% rate, to reach over a $1 million—putting in over $100,000 of your own money. It really is the *time* that compounds the interest that you want on your behalf. That is making your money work for you.

"One great thing about 401(k) plans is that they take money out before tax. So, $100 pre-tax is like $75 after tax if you're in a 25% income tax bracket. Let's say that you put in the $160 per month where there is a 60% match for five years—$100 is your contribution before tax. At the end of five years, with no job change, mathematically the total would be $12,389.90. Then let's say that after graduation you are hired by a company and put $5,000 per year into your 401(k) plan, or $416.67 each month, for another five years, again assuming a 60% match by your employer. At the end of those ten years, you would have $52,650.90. Now let's say you never again put another cent into the plan after the initial ten years. Assuming a mathematical 10% average return for the next ten years, how much would you have when you retire?"

The students started guessing. "$650,000?" … "$300,000?"

"All good guesses, but all of them are too low," the professor said. "Mathematically, you would have $1.04 million before tax and would only have put in a total of $31,000 of your own money."

Many students couldn't believe it.

"Big deal," Malcolm piped up. "Why are you telling us as students to plan for retirement? Isn't that something you should be doing after we have actually finished college and not now?"

"Well," Professor Christensen said with a tone of gratitude. "I want you to consider, if you have the ability, starting to save now. You may wait till you are working, but I want you to learn this now so that you can take full advantage when you start a job."

"Let me explain further," the professor said. "Let's say that you put in the $416.67 per month for 30 years. You would have over $2 million. In contrast, let's say that you didn't start now, but you waited ten years and then started putting in the $416.67 a month and continued for 20 years with that same amount. How much would you have?"

A student made a guess. "One million dollars."

Someone else suggested, "You'd still have two million, minus the twelve thousand."

Another student piped up: "One point five million."

Professor Christensen corrected the students. "You would have $941,878. You see, you cost yourself over a million dollars at the time of retirement by waiting ten years. While it may appear as if it doesn't matter, it's the compounding that you want most. Starting early makes a big difference. The same idea of starting early can work in your 529 Education Savings Account. "This is why Albert Einstein stated, 'Compound interest is the eighth wonder of the world. He, who understands it, earns it; he, who doesn't, pays it.[31]"

Justin raised his hand and said, "Excuse me, Professor. Aren't you predicting that the stocks will always return 10%? I mean, didn't we just have a meltdown in 2008 and 2009? My folks said that during those years, it was all over the news that stock prices went way down and people lost a lot of money. Aren't 401(k) plans tied to stocks?"

Professor Christensen smiled and said, "Yes, they are. To put it simply, if you put $10 in your 401(k), and your employer matched it one-to-one by adding ten dollars, for a total of twenty dollars, the 401(k) plan manager then takes the twenty dollars and invests it in mutual funds. Mutual funds are a collection of stocks managed by a professional team. A mutual fund generally prevents you from keeping all your eggs in one basket. If your

---

31 Einstein, Albert. "Compound interest is the eighth wonder of the world" Good Reads. Accessed August 9, 2017. www.goodreads.com/quotes/76863-compound-interest-is-the-eighth-wonder-of-the-world-he.

account were to lose 50% of its value, you would have ten dollars if you sold during this time. This is why you must average over time.

"When stock prices go down, if you invest the same amount every month, you can buy more shares when the prices are low. When the prices rise, you have added value, provided you didn't sell when the prices were low. This is referred to as *dollar-cost averaging*, where you decide to invest the same amount of money each month and the price averages out over time. People only lost money in the stock market if they sold when the prices were low, or invested in stocks that were overpriced and never returned to previous values. Looking forward to this year, the original values returned to previous and new highs. Additionally, the money that was put in during the time of the fall and rise basically averaged out.

"The question always comes up: 'I don't know what to invest in; where do I start?' Companies know this question will arise, so that's why they created what are called *lifecycle funds,* also known as *target-date funds*. Any reputable, well-known, financial services company can help you find these funds. Check with your plan manager and ask about life-cycle funds, or target date funds. They balance your funds automatically in different types of stocks, bonds, money market funds, and treasury notes, with some even allowing you to invest in both foreign and domestic markets.

"When you're young, you want your money to grow so that it can pay you more money. When you're older, you need to be more conservative, keeping your money from a loss so that you can use it. Lifecycle funds, or target date funds, automatically adjust your investing strategies, and you select them according to when you plan to retire. Professional money managers do most of your investing for you.

"The key is to set it up automatically. It'll be deducted from your paycheck, and you won't even notice it after a while. Set it up once and it's done. Starting early has a big advantage. You can learn more by going to financialmentor.com/calculator/retirement-calculator and cgi.money.cnn.com/tools/savingscalc/savingscalc.htm from Financial Mentor and CNN Money and using their financial calculators.

Managing Taxes—Don't Let Big Amounts Be Taken

"Now let's talk about how to manage taxes," Professor Christensen continued.

"Let's suppose," the professor said, "that you earn $1,000 per month—for easy math. The biggest thing for college students to learn is *cash flow*—where your money flows *from* and where it flows *to*. Most college students don't make enough to pay income taxes at the end of the year, so if you simply go to your human resources department and change your W4 exemptions to a bigger number, you'll have more of your money coming to you. Getting a tax refund means that you gave an interest-free loan to the government. Changing your exemptions will increase your paycheck."

Malcolm spouted out, "How to cheat on taxes! Now, this is my kind of lesson!"

"This is, in fact, very legal," Professor Christensen responded. "Unfortunately, allocating your W4 exemptions and contributing to your 401(k) plan are all part of the game that the present tax code requires that we play."

Justin was beginning to see more clearly the reason to manage taxes and contribute to a 401(k): *prevent unnecessary losses from being deducted so that he could have more available cash.*

"The last thing with tax management," the professor continued, "is to learn to use taxes to your benefit. Keep track of your tuition, books, and housing expenses while in school; you may need them to do your taxes. In a future class, we will be discussing how to use these records of schooling costs to your advantage."

Direct Deposit and High Yield Accounts

"Let's return to the issue of making a return on money by asking a question,"

Professor Christensen said. "Who here would like to make money on their everyday money?"

"Isn't that like asking: 'Who'd like to eat ice cream?'" Maria asked jokingly. "I mean who wouldn't?" Other students nodded in approval.

Professor Christensen smiled, then said, "I want you to open a high-yield savings account, a money market account, an online savings account, or another free account that offers a 'high' rate of return (around 1%), and then direct deposit your paycheck into this account. Look for banks that also offer completely free checking accounts, free online bill payment (often called Bill Pay), mobile deposit, and zero minimum and opening balance requirements."

Justin interjected and asked, "Where would I find a bank that does that? Don't most banks offer around 0.05%? Where do I find a bank to pay me 1%? I don't want to tie my money up in a CD or something that prevents me from actually using my money."

"Great question!" Professor Christensen said as he smiled. "You actually are asking multiple questions, and I will only have the time to discuss some of your implied questions—I'll save the rest for a later class. But first, let me say: You are correct; you may want to avoid CDs right now. The rates are about what you would get with one of the high-yield accounts I mentioned, but the problem is that you tie up your money for long periods of time. A high-yield account is where you would save up your money to get your *diamond*, or the goal that you are saving toward. You can at least pay for some of the sales tax by saving in a high-yield savings account.

"How you find these accounts is by going to your bank and asking about a high-yield savings account and/or money market account. Check out nerdwallet.com/rates/savings-account and money-rates.com/savings.htm to look for these accounts. Some banks will require high initial deposits and high daily balances—you should avoid these places because they will most likely charge you a fee if you don't meet their minimums. Some sample companies might be ally.com, barclays.com, or a local credit union. Generally, avoid institutions that require you to make a certain amount of purchases (as most people end up spending more). Always ask about fees and how to avoid them. Any bank you choose should offer free checking options and allow direct deposit."

"How do I set up direct deposit?" Tyler asked.

"Ask your employer, as each is different, but you will need your account number and bank routing number," Professor Christensen responded. "All of this can be done with your employer. You can set up a high-yield savings account and then have your money automatically put into your account. If your bank offers it, you can use mobile deposit, where an app takes a picture of your check using a smartphone and it is electronically deposited—this will allow you to avoid going to the bank and ensure that you get your money."

Justin remembered the long line he had to wait in at the bank. *Perfect! This will save me time and I don't have to worry about the check clearing in time or catching the bank during business hours. That is awesome.*

"Ask your HR department or supervisor about getting a 401(k), and signing up for direct deposit. Remember the assignment to inquire about tuition assistance or reimbursement. Class dismissed."

Chapter 8: Principles and Suggestions

1. A 401(k) plan gives you free money if your employer matches any portion of your contributions—do this only if you already have college costs covered. If your employer doesn't offer a 401(k) plan, you may consider a Roth IRA. A 401(k) plan is discussed here so you won't leave money on the table and so you get in the habit of saving. Please consider:

   a. Have these contributions automatically made from your paycheck—you may not miss five percent. If done pre-tax, the loss of the money seems easier to bear.
   b. Complete "Understanding Interest" in the workbook.
   c. Consider investing in what are called *target date funds* (also called *lifecycle funds*).

2. Get a free list of banks that have high-yield savings accounts by going to

Nerd Wallet and Money Rates. Some example accounts might be:
a. Ally: ally.com
b. Barclay's: barclays.com
c. A credit union in your area.

Chapter 8: Assignments

1. Ask your HR department or supervisor about:
a. Participating in a 401(k) if your employer offers a match
b. Signing up for direct deposit
c. Changing your W4 deductions to fit your situation—don't leave them at '0' when you can make adjustments. Ask an accountant about your own personal tax situation.
d. Tuition assistance

2. Set up a high-yield savings account that has the option of a free checking account (this will be used in a future chapter). You may need to set up two accounts—the savings account and another for checking. Ensure that the savings account:
a. Has a low required minimum opening balance (under $100)
b. Has no minimum ongoing balance requirement
c. Has at least a 0.75% annual percentage yield
d. Is free (ask about how to avoid fees)
e. Has free online banking and mobile deposit
f. Offers free Bill Pay (will explain in future chapters)

Chapter 8: Warnings and What to Avoid

1. Avoid accounts that require you to spend certain amounts or make a certain number of transactions (e.g., one that offers 2% if you make 15 transactions per month at a physical register). Often these types of accounts will often encourage spending more, or have stipulations that if you fail to meet their exact requirements, your return is reduced to about 0.05%.

2. Some high-yield accounts may require you only to make a certain number of withdrawals—future chapters will discuss this. There are ways around this requirement—just be aware that high yield savings accounts may limit the number of withdrawals you can do each month.

3. The stock market can go down, affecting your 529 Education Savings Plan or 401(k) plan. Speak with the financial advisor for your plan. Target-date or lifecycle funds can be good options to automatically govern your money with deadline-appropriate funds, but even these can have risk associated.

Chapter 9
Making it Happen—
Finances

Justin liked Professor Christensen's idea of being rewarded on money you already earn. Since he was really quite impressed with what Professor Christensen said was available for payment options, he decided that he would put the professor's principles to the test.

Fixed Expenses and Fluctuating Expenses

At work, Justin got an email from Professor Christensen:

Class,

In addition to managing taxes, contacting the human resources rep about 401(k), and opening a high-yield account, I want you to divide your expenses into fixed and fluctuating categories. We didn't get to this concept in class.

Rent, car insurance, health insurance, etc. are fixed expenses. Food, gasoline, fun, utilities, or anything else that varies is a fluctuating expense. Your cell phone depending upon your plan could be in either category. Basically, anything that doesn't change amounts over a repeatable period is a fixed expense. Please DON'T send me the amounts, just the categories.

*For now, DON'T worry about tuition and books in these calcula-
tions. Submit this info along with the other assignments on the class
website before our next class.*

Sincerely,
Professor Christensen

After reading the email, Justin started began working on his homework.
First, Justin applied for another scholarship at work. Justin had written a
paper for another class and he really liked the idea of turning every college
paper and essay that he had written into a potential scholarship. It sort of
gave him a monetary value for his papers, and it made them a lot more
enjoyable to do. This also helped him apply faster. It had been several weeks
since Justin was awarded a scholarship, but he was still hopeful.

Inquiring about High-Yield Accounts

Justin decided that he would work on the banking part of the homework
next. He went to his bank's website and after he authenticated, chatted with
an online customer service representative.

[**Justin**] I would like to know about money market accounts.

[**Rep**] Yes, we have those. What do you want to know?

[**Justin**] Is there a minimum balance that is required?

[**Rep**] Do you mean to open an account, or for daily transactions?

[**Justin**] Both.

[**Rep**] There is a $10,000 minimum to open, and you must maintain
a daily balance of at least $5,000.

[**Justin**] How many transactions are allowed?

[**Rep**] We allow six withdrawals and unlimited deposits each month.

[**Justin**] Just curious—why are the opening and daily balances so high when companies like Ally or ones found on Nerd Wallet and Money Rates offer money market accounts for *no* minimum balances?

[**Rep**] Let me put it this way: Our bank is in the business of making money. We only make money if certain balances are achieved.

Justin was a little taken aback. *Are you literally telling me that you are knowingly ripping me off? At whose expense are you achieving these balances?* Justin kept his responses pleasant.

[**Justin**] How do companies like Ally make money then?

[**Rep**] I don't know their business plan, but they have fewer buildings and less staff. You may get bad customer service.

[**Justin**] Can you match their savings products with lower opening minimums and no daily balance minimum—while still allowing me to get a higher interest rate?

[**Rep**] No.

[**Justin**] Can you tell me any advantage of choosing the service you offer over the services of Ally or Barclay's or any other bank found through Nerd Wallet?

[**Rep**] You can have all of your banking in one place.

[**Justin**] I can link accounts to send and receive money automatically. Why would banking in one place help me, when you require such high minimum balances?

[**Rep**] Look, I don't make the rules. I just help people get what they need. We offer quality products to help our customers; if you don't want to take advantage of them, that is fine.

[**Justin**] Okay, thanks.[32]

Every business is in the business of making money, Justin thought. *Why else be in business? If that is how a representative of my bank treats me, I think other businesses can at least treat me with courtesy. The representative's information might be only somewhat accurate. While it might be true that companies like Ally or Barclay's have fewer buildings, the customer service might be just as good, if not better than, my current bank's customer service, plus I can do everything online.* Justin felt justified in going to another bank.

He went to ally.com and set up a high-yield savings account and a checking account. He had to link his new accounts to his checking account. He did an initial funding which would take two business days to finalize, and he would not be able to withdraw the money for five business days after his initial deposit. However, Justin could immediately use direct deposit of his wages into his new money market account. He sent an email to his boss, Kevin, asking if he could set up direct deposit, and whether any tuition assistance or reimbursement was available, and whether there was a 401(k) available to him. Justin had heard Kevin mention direct deposit a few times but had never taken the time to set it up.

Set Up Direct Deposit and Change Exemptions

At home, Justin checked his email and found that Kevin had answered. He described how to set up direct deposit and said that Justin needed to know his account and routing numbers. Kevin also provided a link to set this up. He said that SSU only allowed full-time employees to contribute to a 401(k) or get tuition covered by the university. So, those options weren't available to Justin. *This is a first. Professor Christensen's advice didn't work for me. At least I get direct deposit.*

Justin logged into his new high-yield savings account with Ally and then clicked the link that Kevin had provided in his e-mail. He entered his

---

32 Similar to a real phone conversation the author had with a bank about fees. However, DO CHECK with your bank to see if they have competitive products.

banking information into his employee portal and saved it there. *No more going to the bank to cash my paycheck. This will be perfect!* Justin noticed up to seven different accounts could be used for direct deposit, which would allow him to divide his paycheck into different accounts however he wanted. *Hmmm…I wonder how I could take advantage of that?*

While in his employee portal, Justin noticed a link that read "exemptions." *I wonder…* He clicked the link and found, not surprisingly, no exemptions. There was a questionnaire, and after answering it, Justin learned that he could rightfully claim a few exemptions, or deductible entries in the dependents' field, as allowed by law on his W-4 form.[33] After he clicked on "submit," the employee portal indicated that he would be sending his money to Ally bank and getting a bigger paycheck by not having as much tax deducted.

Benefits of Applying to Scholarships

The next day, Justin checked his email and found an email about a scholarship for which he had applied earlier in the semester. Justin had gotten used to these emails and letters; he had probably a dozen of them. The letters and emails would usually thank him for his submission and notify him that he had not been selected. Some would encourage him to apply again. It was kind of frustrating. Justin clicked the email and saw that it read:

> *Congratulations Mr. Murray,*
>
> *You have been awarded a $2,000 scholarship. The money has been sent to your campus's tuition department. You should see the money in the next* three to six *business days….*
>
> Justin was elated. *Holy cow! A free $2,000; that is incredible.* Justin did

---

33 Every W-4 form has a questionnaire for adding up legal dependents and exemptions. Please check your employer's payroll department (usually HR) so that more taxes than you will owe are not deducted. You may also want to consult an accountant.

a quick calculation: *I have spent less than 21 hours applying for scholarships: $2,000/21 hours ≅ $95 per hour. I was paid $95 PER HOUR?!! That is amazing. Where else would I get paid that much—especially for just using my school essays and projects? Even though I have applied to 14 scholarships, getting just one makes it totally worth it.* Justin said a quick prayer and expressed gratitude for the scholarship and all the people who had helped him.

Based on his previous experience, Justin knew that the surplus money would be offered to him from the tuition office as a check. Now that he had Ally for a bank, he wouldn't have to cash the check, as his phone had mobile deposit.

Justin went to the food court, hoping to run into Allison. On his way, Justin noticed an information booth that had a sign displaying an ad for "Free Corn Maze Tickets." It explained that a farmer had created a maze in the dry stalks of his corn and was inviting people to come. The corn maze sounded like fun and he grabbed a few tickets. Justin then went to the food court; he was in luck! Allison was at the register.

"Hey, Justin," Allison said with a smile.

"How's it going?" Justin asked.

"Fine," said Allison.

"Could I get a small loaf of wheat bread with some honey butter?" Justin asked.

"Sure thing," Allison responded. As she was getting the bread, she asked. "Have you started on the homework yet?"

"Yeah," he answered. "Yesterday, I opened a high-yield savings account, started direct deposit, and changed my W4 exemptions."

"Good job!" said Allison. "You're almost done. It sounds like you just need to do, what was it...? Separate your fixed expenses from your fluctuating ones."

"Yeah, that's right," Justin said half-assuring, half-questioning. "What do you think that Professor Christensen is going to have us do with that separation?"

"I don't know, but he obviously has something in mind," Allison replied. "I mean, I wouldn't have been awarded any scholarships if I hadn't applied because Professor Christensen had taught us to. Plus his scholarship equation really helped a lot."

"You got a scholarship?! Congratulations! I just got another one. It's amazing to see how much you get paid per hour; I added up my time spent applying for all the scholarships and I made over $95 per hour by getting just the one."

"That's crazy, isn't it?" Allison commented.

Justin then asked Allison how *she* was doing on the homework.

401(k) Benefits and Tuition Reimbursement

"You're not going to believe this," Allison said. "I checked at work to see if they have a 401(k) program and any tuition assistance, and I was surprised; they have both."

"Wait—the school doesn't have a 401(k) program. I checked," Justin said.

"I meant," said Allison, correcting him, "my other job at the hotel. You probably don't remember, but I'm working two jobs."

"Oh," said Justin.

Allison continued. "It turns out they offer 100% 401(k) matching up to four percent of my total paycheck. And they offer $1,000 of tuition reimbursement every six months after you've worked there for a minimum of two months. Since I started the job in the summer, I'm just barely eligible. I spoke with my human resources contact and started the reimbursement process for summer classes. Can you believe that?!"

"That's great!" said Justin.

"I get summer classes reimbursed from tuition reimbursement—plus, an additional four percent of my paycheck if I start contributing to my 401(k) plan!" Allison said excitedly.

"So did you sign up?" Justin asked with joking curiosity.

"Of course!" replied Allison. "I had my notes in my backpack when I called my human resources contact, and I asked about target date funds. The HR representative said those were standard. He sent me to the company intranet to see the forms for both the 401(k) and the tuition reimbursement. I filled them out electronically and sent them in. Starting next paycheck, I'll be contributing six percent, to make an even ten percent—I figured with the $1,000 dollars for tuition reimbursement, I was able to route some of my paycheck to be saved—especially when it's matched by my employer."

"That was nice."

"It sure was!" Then Allison handed Justin his warm bread. "Here's your bread."

They had been engrossed in their conversation and didn't realize they were holding up the line. Justin paid and left to eat his bread.

"Real quick," Justin said returning to face Allison again.

"Yeah. What is it?" Allison responded with a smile.

"I got some tickets to go to a corn maze and wondered if you'd like to go with me this Saturday at 6 p.m."

"Sounds fun, I'll see you then," Allison said handing Justin his receipt he had forgotten.

That afternoon at work, Justin quickly submitted another scholarship application. He wanted in on this free money deal both he and Allison had gotten. *Allison got hooked up*, Justin thought. *I wish I could have a job like that.* He was a little envious of her getting tuition reimbursement and 401(k) money. *Free money. Hmmm, that sounds even better than free pizza.* Justin was grateful that his job at least allowed him to do his homework—and he had gotten $2,000. Justin then sent an email to Bob, the program advisor whom he had met when he first came to SSU, asking if there were any additional scholarships being offered for his major. He was excited to start earning interest on his money while he saved up for next semester's tuition and his trip to Chichen Itza.

Adding Up Fixed and Fluctuating Expenses

Justin decided it would only take him a few minutes to add up his fixed and fluctuating expenses. So he pulled out a blank sheet of paper and started making lists in two columns.

Let's see, he began. *There are rent, electricity, food, car expenses.* Justin realized that, as he was becoming more aware of what he spent his money on, that he had to create more categories. *Wait—Let me be specific.* Crossing out "car expenses," Justin replaced it with "gasoline," "maintenance costs," and "average monthly insurance costs." *What else? Ah yes, cell phone, part of the internet bill at home, fun, date money, and miscellaneous items. I don't need to worry now about books, tuition, and class fees. Is that everything? No, there's more: tithing (as its own category), heat at my apartment, and my portion of the water bill. No health insurance because I'm still covered by mom and dad's policy. I think that's all.*

Now, what are fixed expenses? Justin decided to write next to each item whether it was a fixed expense or fluctuating one, and then type it up to clean it up. *Rent, car insurance, cell phone plan, my part of the internet, and the water bill are fixed costs.*

My portions of electricity and heat, food, gasoline, maintenance costs, fun, date money, and miscellaneous items are my fluctuating expenses. Justin knew that he did not need to submit the amounts, but he was curious. Justin opened his credit card statement and looked at locations where he was spending cash. He tried to assign approximate values to each category. Very quickly he could answer how much he was spending on his fixed expenses. *That was easier than I thought.* Some of his fluctuating expenses were more difficult. Some of the expenses shocked Justin, such as his gasoline being $87.13 for the last month. *Holy cow! What am I doing spending that much when I work on campus? No wonder Professor Christensen wanted us to write up our expenses. One of his purposes may have been to help us become aware of where we are spending money.*

Justin typed up his fixed and fluctuating expenses (without his amounts, although he now knew his total expenses for both fixed and fluctuating expenses).

Chapter 9: Principles and Suggestions

1. Start earning money on your income by setting up a high-yield savings account.

2. Check with your employer about direct deposit, tuition reimbursement, 401(k) contributions, and W4 tax allocations.

3. Applying to multiple scholarships is like getting paid $10 to $500 per hour. They really do pay off.

Chapter 9: Assignments

1. List your expenses in categories.

2. Designate each expense category as fixed or fluctuating.

3. Separately total your fixed expenses and fluctuating expenses. If you find that you are spending too much in one category, this may be a good time to consider your *bubblegum-diamond-thieves* as mentioned in Chapter 7.

4. Complete the "Common College Money Traps" exercise in the workbook.

5. Complete the "Fixed Versus Fluctuating Expenses" exercise.

Chapter 9: Warnings and What to Avoid

1. Don't get discouraged if it seems that applying to scholarships is not working out, or if every principle taught cannot be applied to you. Become aware of what is available to you and use that to your advantage. The more you practice, the more you can improve, and eventually win.

2. The biggest problem that most people face is either not knowing about a solution, or not taking action to implement it. You now know many of the solutions; how are you doing on implementing them?

Chapter 10
Money Channels

Justin was excited to attend the next class. When he got there, he and Allison talked a bit before class began. Allison had similar success—she was awarded a Pell Grant by applying with the FAFSA, had some scholarships, tuition reimbursement, and a 401(k), and was saving money in a high-yield account.

Professor Christensen began class by saying, "Good work everyone. Most of you checked with employers for 401(k) plans and tuition assistance, and looked into tax exemptions. Additionally, you should have added up your fixed and fluctuating expenses. Let's add a few more parts and you'll be set. I think you are going to like this next part."

At the reference to fixed and fluctuating expenses, Justin remembered he had forgotten to submit that part of the assignment. *Aww snap. I completely forgot. Professor Christensen is going to give me a '0.' This is going to kill my grade.*

Professor Christensen continued, interrupting Justin's thoughts.

Avoiding Debt with Your Fluctuating Expenses

"Now, for your homework, most of you submitted your categories of fixed and fluctuating expenses," Professor Christensen said.

Justin silently groaned.

"Let me tell you a strategy to help you avoid debt on day-to-day expenses," Professor Christensen continued. "Now that you know the fluctuating expenses, get a reloadable prepaid debit card or make modifications to a dedicated checking account that has a debit card. I recommend that you two or four times per month, set up automatic transfers from another checking or savings account. It is best if you can set up specific days that it will arrive by. Generally, it takes three business days to complete a transfer from one bank to another. For example, if you want your money to be there on the 1st and the 15th of the month, set up an automatic transfer to leave your high-yield account on the 10th and the 23rd. The extra days allow for weekends, holidays, and short months. If you have two checking accounts with the same bank, the transfer can happen almost instantly. In this scenario, the best thing to do is have some of your utilities (like your heating or electric bill) draft on the 1st and other utilities to draft on the 15th (like a pay-as-you-go cell phone). That way, you will be sure to have the money in your account for your utilities.

"If you would like to use a bank's debit card instead of a reloadable prepaid debit card, you need to ask your bank how you can put this one condition on the checking account you will use: If there is not enough money in the account, deny the charge. The bank will have you fill out one to three forms. Complete these and then when you use your debit card, when you go to check out at the gas station or supermarket and you don't have enough money on the card, the card will deny the purchase request. Without this, if you go over the amount in your checking account with a standard debit card, you get fined. This written request with the bank prevents you from overspending and saves you overdraft fees that are about $40–$80 a pop, plus interest."

"You mean banks will charge me if I go over my account balance if I use a regular debit card?" Maria asked.

"Both fees and interest," Professor Christensen said. "This is kind of sad, but true."

"That is so stupid," Allison said. "Why don't they just deny the charge? It seems that they're only after your money."

"You should know," the professor said, "with either the prepaid debit card or the bank debit card, this will _not_ work if you use your debit card as a credit card when you check out, or if you set up recurring payments using your special debit card."

"Excuse me, professor," Maria politely interjected. "Why would I want to put my fluctuating expenses on a debit card that has limits compared to just using cash? Why is this beneficial to me?"

"That is a great question and what I was about to explain." Professor Christensen answered.

"Sorry," Maria remarked.

"Don't be," he continued, "not understanding something is why you should ask for clarification."

Addressing the class, Professor Christensen asked, "Has anyone ever seen the envelope system, where people put money into different envelopes for different categories of expenses, and then spend the money in that envelope (for example, food, gas, etc.)? Once it's gone, it's gone."

Several students nodded in acknowledgment.

"First, what's good about that system?" the professor asked.

Students began to shout out answers: "Keeps you in check so you don't overspend," "Keeps you aware of your money," "Helps you budget."

"Good!" Professor Christensen said. "I agree with all of those answers. Now, what are some negatives to that system?"

Students again answered "If you lose your money or get mugged, you are hosed because you aren't likely to get it back," "You must keep counting out your money each month—it gets tedious and many people don't keep this up," and "It is hard for people to pull the correct amount of money from the correct envelope like going to the grocery store and buying food and toiletries," were some of the replies.

"Very good job," Professor Christensen said. "May I add two more to the list?" Some students nodded in approval. "First, there is no automatic record-keeping: If you pay with cash, and lose the receipt, you will have a very difficult time trying to figure out how much you spent and where.

Second, there are no safety protections against someone getting your cash and spending it without your permission.

"This is where the special debit card comes in. You get almost all of the benefits of the envelope system and none of the negatives. With your special debit card, you can keep yourself from overspending by not exceeding your card balance. When you make a purchase, it automatically records the date, the amount, the merchant, and often a reference code for you automatically—you don't have to write down your transactions. It is also secure. If someone uses your card fraudulently, the bank reimburses you. If you lose your card or it is stolen, you can, within minutes, deactivate your card and be issued a new one. And best of all, you can reload the card automatically from another account."

"What about certain stores or warehouse clubs that only accept one brand of card?" Tyler asked. "Does this mean that I'll need different cards for each store?"

"Great question!" Professor Christensen responded. "Let me share two more benefits that I didn't mention. First, most stores, even if they don't accept credit cards, will accept debit cards, regardless of the card issuer. This means that they can be accepted at those stores you mentioned. Second, just like reward credit cards, there are reward debit cards that will give 0.5% to 2.5% rewards."

"That is so cool," Tyler said. "I didn't know that."

Professor Christensen continued, "Because you added up all your fluctuating expenses, you know your total amount of expenses. You can automatically transfer money onto your special debit card two or four times per month on the days you choose. The written request to deny the charge if there is not enough money will save you overdraft fees and prevent you from going over your limits. You also need to follow this one rule: If you spend too much money in one area, you must make up for it in other areas. If you run your AC all month and have a big electric bill, you must decrease your fun and buy cheaper food. If you spend too much on dates, you must park your car and walk to avoid paying for gasoline. Each category in the fluctuating expenses amount can compensate for the rest."

"That seems really easy," Justin said, "a lot easier than having to stuff envelopes with money or write down every expense. And the money gets to your account automatically, so you don't have to think about it?!"

"I'm glad you think so because your next assignment will be to go to a bank and inquire about having an account that denies the purchase if the amount exceeds the balance, or getting a pre-paid debit card." Professor Christensen said sunnily.

"I knew there was a reason you were asking us to add up our fluctuating expenses," Malcolm said exasperatedly.

"You caught me," Professor Christensen said cheerfully. "To aid in this assignment, I suggest you look at ally.com, barclays.com, or another one from Nerd Wallet."

"Wait!" Allison said. "If that was the purpose for the fluctuating expenses, what was the reason for the fixed expenses?"

"Ah, Ms. Pratt, your observation is astute. Very perceptive of you." The professor said. "I do have something in mind for that."

How to Use Bill Pay—Automatically Paying Bills

"Has anyone heard of Bill Pay?" the professor asked.

A few people raised their hands.

"Well," said the professor, "for those of you don't know what it is, Bill Pay—or online bill payment, is generally a free service through your bank that will send out a certified check or electronic payment to a person or an institution you owe money to, to arrive by a date that you select.

"You simply submit the name of the business (or person), as well as your name and account number with that business, and your bank will print all the information on the check when it's sent. You will set up whatever recurring schedule you need for each check: monthly, quarterly, annually, or you can set up a one-time payment. So with Bill Pay, you can have your bills paid automatically. It automates your finances.

"Has anyone ever used Bill Pay, or any other free bill payment app?" Professor Christensen asked. A few people raised their hands.

"Well, good! Some of you are familiar with the process," he exclaimed. "Using Bill Pay allows you to keep control of your payments and know exactly how much your total payments are each month. If you use the electronic option, it can send your payments almost instantly—one or two days before they are due.

"Ultimately, what happens is that you pay your fixed expenses using a free bill payment service. You no longer have to worry about payment of your fixed bills. They get paid on time automatically.

"Of course, you must notify Bill Pay of the date you want the check to arrive at the recipient. Bear in mind that it usually takes five business days for the bank to have the check arrive (including printing and mailing time) to where you owe money. So, knowing the date you would like the check to be delivered, count backward six to seven business days so that the funds can settle, and that will be the day that you'll need to have money in your account to provide an extra cushion—in case there is a holiday or weekend. The easy way to do this is to check with your bank and ask what you need to do to ensure that your payments to arrive by a certain date, including weekends and holidays. Then set up a recurring transfer from your high-yield savings account to occur the day before."

"Wait!?" Justin asked.

"Yes," said Professor Christensen said.

"What about allowing my rent to be automatically deducted from my checking account?"

"Well, that can be an option—and it is a good option if you are paying a mortgage," Professor Christensen replied. "However, for renting it may be a different story; to do an automatic withdrawal you must give your account information to your landlord and you give the landlord control of your payment ability. Banks have to comply with stringent regulations to be allowed to handle your money, but landlords don't have to comply with those same regulations.[34] When you are a student, if the spring semester ends on May 10th, the landlord or property manager may take all of your rent for the month; not take any rent, expecting you to pay by check personally, or something else. Ask the landlord what security measures are in place and what happens at the end of semesters when there is a partial month. If the landlord uses a third-party company, this can be better than just giving the money directly. Then ask the landlord to email you a receipt.[35] This way you remain in control, and you can stop the payment if necessary and prevent landlords from stealing your money or making a mistake."

"I never thought of that," Justin said. "Bill Pay does seem nice."

"It allows you to automatically pay your fixed expenses on time and keep control of your money," the professor repeated.

Future Expenses

"Class," Professor Christensen said, "do you remember how I told you about *bubblegum-diamond-thieves*?"

Several class members nodded.

"Well, as part of that we discussed eliminating unnecessary expenses and not wasting money. Another part of it was saving up your money for something you value. Well, if you have a big bill coming up like tuition, you should save up the money first and then pay it. This allows you to avoid paying interest and gives you additional options.

"This semester," the professor continued, "you should set a goal to save up all of your tuition and book costs by the end of the semester, as well as

---

34 Some states have laws that prohibit landlords from taking money out of your account because there were disputes about the landlord taking too much. Some landlords or property managers are dishonest. It may be better to use Bill Pay—it is free and is a good paper or electronic option.

35 NOTE: If rent is due on the 5th, have your Bill Pay payment arrive on the 1st or 2nd day of the month. Ask the manager or landlord to email you a receipt.

your first month's living expenses. I know you are all applying to scholarships—and if you keep up applying to at least two per week, you will have greater chances of success by applying to at least thirty scholarships over the semester. Additionally, if you will use the Utah 529 Education Savings Plan, you can get a state income tax credit, as long as you are working in the state. Keep working at any jobs that you can. Use every resource you can to help pay for college. I highly recommend that you limit your expenses—especially selling your car to pay for your education. The rewards to doing these things are that you can enter the job market, start your own business, or go on to graduate school without the weight of debt. You will have freedom, and can start ahead of your peers."

Justin really liked the sound of freedom. It made him feel good to be free—to have choices.

"Some students," Professor Christensen said, "get massive student loans and then cannot get a job. These student loans follow them for decades, and they eventually default, which really hurts them in the future. College is a time to learn and prepare. It is a time to decide who you want to be. Most students who have trouble with student loans are using the money to buy things they cannot afford. They go to schools that are too expensive, they live in expensive housing, they party, they don't control their purchases, and they live it up.

"Remember, it is not what you make, but what you keep, that matters. This principle of saving up for your expenses will bless you your entire life.

The assignments for today are to one, do an internet search and find a 529 Education Savings Plan—call a support number from the official site and ask the questions about 529 Education Savings Plans we discussed; two, decide on either a prepaid debit card or special debit card by talking to your bank; three, inquire with your bank about a free online bill payment service, like Bill Pay, for your fixed expenses—but *DON'T* set it up yet. Class dismissed."

Overcoming Setbacks

After class, Justin went up to Professor Christensen. "I was wondering about the assignment to add up my fixed and fluctuating expenses. I had so many things going on, I did the assignment," he said, showing Professor Christensen the completed hand-sketched results, "and I meant to submit it after work, but I completely forgot. Could I still get credit for the assignment if I submit it now?"

"The good news is, Justin," Professor Christensen empathetically, "you will still be able to do the assignment. In fact, it is still required for the money channels assignment. The bad news is that for that part of the assignment, you will be getting a '0.' If you had an illness or school-excused absence, I could've been lenient, but since you didn't, unfortunately, this assignment will get a '0.' I have to be fair to the other class members who submitted the assignment on time. You know the class rules about submitting on time. But don't worry, you will still be able to get an 'A' in the class if you don't let this happen again and submit every assignment on time. You are doing really well. *Don't let a simple slip up destroy everything you have worked towards.* Learn from it, make corrections, and do better from here on out. You are still a good student."

Justin left feeling both discouraged at missing an assignment and happy that Professor Christensen had paid him a compliment. *I guess I deserve that '0.' But it still irks me that I missed a simple assignment. Professor Christensen was really nice about it, he even paid me a compliment, but I definitely don't want to make that mistake again.*

Chapter 10: Principles and Suggestions

1. Control your day-to-day (fluctuating) expenses using your prepaid debit card or special debit card from a specific account from your bank.

2. Bill Pay allows you to send money to people or organizations either electronically or by a mailed paper check. Bill Pay can be a great asset to help you simplify your life and pay bills on time.

    a.   Paying rent with an automatic withdrawal from the landlord could be bad or good—it depends on the landlord. The best option is to issue a payment from Bill Pay electronically.

3. If you have a big expense coming up (e.g., tuition) save up for it in advance. You can save a lot of fees and interest this way.

4. If you make a mistake, learn from it, and avoid repeating it.

Chapter 10: Assignments

1. Do one of the following for your fluctuating expenses:
   a.   Go to Nerd Wallet and look for a reloadable, prepaid debit card. Inquire about setting a card up.
   b.   (Better option) Go to ally.com or barclays.com, and set up a specific checking account that is dedicated to fixed expenses. Call and ask a bank representative how to make the account and related debit cards deny the charge (without a fee) if there is not enough money in the account. Fill out all paperwork. This option is better because you can more easily have control over the debit card, reissue a new card if ever needed, and, when you get married, add a spouse to the account and get a second debit card.

2. Look at your fixed expenses (from Chapters 8 and 9) and contact the organizations or people that you pay a fixed amount of money to on a reoccurring basis. Ask them:
   a.   Can I schedule my bill to come on the same day of the month?
   b.   Do you accept electronic payments from a bank through Bill Pay? If so how do I set this up? If not, how do I send you a check in the mail for my account?
   c.   Do you accept credit cards for payment? If so, is there a fee?
   d.   After I send a payment, will you send me an email confirming that you got my payment?

3. Complete the "Calculating Costs" exercise in the workbook.

4. Complete the "Eliminating Expenses and Amplifying Income" exercises in the workbook.

5. Make a commitment to save up the money for your future expenses. Work jobs, get scholarships, use FAFSA, use 529 Education Savings Plans, and use every other resource you can.

Chapter 10: Warnings and What to Avoid

1. With the special or prepaid debit card, there still can be overage charges if you use an automatic payment (e.g., your electric bill) or use the card as a credit card; ALWAYS select debit card when paying. Also, have your bills come at certain days after you transfer money to your special debit card or prepaid debit card (e.g., if your electric bill is due by the 3rd of each month and your internet bill is due by the 17th, transfer money to arrive by the 1st and 15th).

Chapter 11
Simplifying Finances

At a break between classes, Justin logged into his account with Ally. He began a chat with a representative. Justin asked about setting up a separate account that would be used to control expenses with his debit card.

Special Checking Account and Debit Card Setup

Justin decided to ask Ally if they would deny charges similar to what Professor Christensen had suggested. After chatting with a representative and explaining what he wanted to do, the representative from Ally informed Justin that that feature wasn't available.

"Thanks anyway," Justin typed in reply. "I would like to make Ally my primary bank account, but use another account (or prepaid debit card) that would allow me to have charges be denied without a fee to prevent overspending. Will you please suggest the feature?"

"I will make the suggestion," the representative typed as they ended the chat session.

Drat, Justin thought, *it would be so much easier to just use one bank so I could more easily transfer between accounts.*[36] *I will contact my bank and see if they have the ability to deny charges if there is not enough money, and if they don't, I can find another bank or get a pre-paid debit card.* Justin logged into the bank that he used for the past few years and started chatting.

---

36 If you can find a bank that has no fees, a high-yield savings account, and has the option of denying charges if requested, pick that bank as transfers will happen closer.

[**Justin**] Hello. I'd like to find out about if my checking account can deny a charge if there is not enough money in the account—not overdraft protection, but actually deny the purchase, without a fee, if there are insufficient funds, when I use my debit card.

[**Rep**] Yes, our bank allows our checking accounts to have a rule setup that would deny charges if there is not enough money in the account. However, you should know that if you establish overdraft protection, use your debit card like a credit card by selecting "credit" at a store, write a check that exceeds the balance, or have a recurring charge (one that has been given permission to automatically withdraw money—like paying your monthly cellphone bill), that you will be assessed a fee of $40 for each of those types of charges. Aside from those, if you setup the rule, then yes, your debit card purchase will be denied if you do not have enough money in the checking account.

[**Justin**] Great. How do I set this up? Are there really no fees?

[**Rep**] Come into a branch and fill out the forms. There's no fee as long as you sign up and use your debit card as a debit card.

[**Justin**] Thanks. I will stop by the branch by my college shortly.

Justin later went to the campus branch of his physical bank, and filled out the forms to authorize his checking account to deny the charges if there was not enough money in the account. He was politely reminded what the rep had said that the bank would only deny the charges if he used his debit card as a debit card, didn't use checks, didn't have recurring charges on his account, and ended his over-draft protection (which he previously had enabled).

Justin had previously estimated that he would spend no more than $285 per month on fluctuating expenses: $150 for food, $80 for gasoline, and $35 for his portion of electricity, gas, and internet. If he had any money left over from his food or gasoline allotments, he could spend that on fun and activities, but no more. He then added together the categories of fluctuating expenses, tithing, and fixed expenses, and arranged to have half the total amount transferred from his money market account to his Ally checking account on the 25th (accounting for February) and 11th of each month, so that he would be able to transfer the money from to his Ally checking account to his newly converted special debit account, by the 1st and 15th of each month, and the other half by the 15th.

Justin couldn't help thinking about the gasoline and insurance costs for his car. *I'd be saving well over $200 per month if I were to sell my car, but I'm going to hold off on that for now.*

Inquiring about Bill Pay

Justin called the property management company he paid rent to and got the information about paying rent on a recurring basis. "Yes, we take credit cards, but we charge a $25 fee to do so," the representative said. She went on to explain that there was an electronic option. "You just need to put your account ID in the payment info notes," she said. After getting the information, Justin was told how to go to the account portal to view his statement. Justin asked if he could be emailed when the money arrived. "I can set that up," the rep responded.

Justin realized that if he set up the electronic payment option to arrive by the first day of each month, he needed to have money to pay rent transferred to his Ally checking account; he could add this amount to the money coming out on the 25th for his fluctuating expenses. [37] This allowed Justin to transfer his rent, fluctuating expenses, and fixed expenses in one lump sum from his high-yield savings account with Ally.

That was easier than I thought it would be, Justin mused. After contacting

---

37 If you find a bank that can meet the criterion for having a high-yield account, allows you to have multiple checking accounts, and has rules to deny debit card purchases if there is not enough money in the account, then the same thing can be accomplished by having the money transferred instantly on the 1st and 15th using an ACH for rent.

each of the organizations that he did business with, he found that most of them did have the credit card option without a fee.

Using 529 Education Savings Plans

When he was done, Justin decided to go online and learn more about the Utah Educational Savings Plan (UESP). Justin went to *www.uesp.org* and found that the plan had low fees, and the money could be used at any accredited educational institution. Additionally, since he was now working in Utah, he could claim a statewide tax credit of five percent.

What caught Justin's attention were the age-based funds, the funds similar to the lifecycle funds or target date funds mentioned by Professor Christensen. He read over the online handout and found that lifecycle funds would automatically take care of diversification and allocation of money and cycle the money for different periods. Since he was a freshman, he would need some of the money for the current semester and he could grow his money for his junior and senior years by investing in target-date funds. When Justin was finally ready to use his money someday, the handout said, he'd want it mostly in money market accounts.

Justin, at this point, was at a loss. *Should I put my money in a Roth IRA and not access it for years, or should I put it in an educational savings plan and get a low return?* He concluded that he needed to better define his goals and get more information. He decided to take a five-minute break, so between class periods, he put up a sign on the desk saying "Back in 5 min."

Justin called the UESP contact number. He asked the representative for which expenses the plan could be used.

"The Utah Educational Savings Plan can be used at any accredited educational institution in the USA for tuition, the actual cost of books, room and board, and lab or class fees," the receptionist said.

"Are there any special benefits for me if I work in Utah?" Justin asked.

"You can get a five percent state credit on your taxes, up to the set limit," the receptionist said.

"If I wanted to use the money in less than three years, what should I invest in to keep my money safe?" Justin asked.

"I cannot give financial or legal advice," the receptionist responded. "However, I can connect you with a plan-sponsored financial planner."

"That would be great," Justin said.

The receptionist put him through to the financial planner. Justin explained his dilemma, stating that he wanted the money to be available in less than three years.

"Keep in mind," said the financial planner, "that you get a five percent state income tax credit for working in Utah. That is like getting a five percent return on your money simply because you saved it. To make things a little better for you, why don't you invest in … ?" The financial planner gave Justin a plan that would allow his money to grow and told him which funds would give him the best return for such a short period of time while remaining as safe as possible.

"Remember," the financial advisor added, "the returns aren't guaranteed. They can go down, but that is a fairly safe plan for a one-, two-, and three-year outlook, and you can still get the tax credit on top of it. Even though the return will probably be less than two percent, that is still better than most CDs or money market accounts. Just be sure to use the money only for qualified expenses, and you'll be fine. The money won't be taxed when you take it out—including any growth—as long as you use it on qualified expenses."

Justin thanked the financial planner for his time.

Justin reviewed the goals he had made earlier: going to Chichen Itza and graduating without credit card or student loan debt. *If I set a goal to continue to save for Chichen Itza, I'll get five percent credited from what I would have spent on state income tax, plus what I can get on my return from investing, and I can use the money for the most expensive parts of a college education—including housing,* Justin mused. *As long as I continue to save in my money market account, that is the route for me,* he concluded. He went back to work and signed up for the UESP 529.[38]

---

38 See *Finding College Cash: Real Estate* to learn more.

As part of the savings plan, Justin decided to put in $1,000 to start. He linked the plan to his checking account. The money was withdrawn and the funds were processed. Justin then remembered that the last part of the assignment was to automate all of his finances. He thought about how Allison was able to automatically contribute to her 401(k) plan from her paycheck. He went back to the rules for his 529 ESP and looked for the info. Sure enough, he could contribute to his 529 plan directly from his paycheck in the same way that direct deposits were done at the bank.

I get paid twice per month, so if I just set up a contribution of $200 per paycheck to the savings plan and contribute money from scholarships, I can have all the money I need or use the money for tuition. Justin logged into his email and clicked the link that Kevin, his boss, had given him, which led him back to his employee portal. He added the account information for the newly formed UESP and set up an automatic $200 deposit from each paycheck into the plan.

Justin was already seeing results from automating his financial matters. Honestly, he felt a little excited to just get everything done so that it didn't require a lot of maintenance and upkeep. Justin wanted to focus on school, and it was nice to know that his finances were being automated.

Justin submitted his breakdown of fluctuating expenses and fixed expenses—the one he had done before but forgotten to submit. He then submitted his findings about the 529 Education Savings Plan in a statement he wrote about setting up the account for the fixed expenses and fluctuating expenses. Justin also wrote what he had done in relation to Bill Pay. *I can tell that I am automating expenses and these are the parts that I do not yet know, but I can see the value in having all of my expenses paid automatically.*

Tomorrow, I am seeing Allison at a corn maze.

Cash Conversations—Good Principles to Live By

At the corn maze, Justin and Allison tried to see how lost they could get in the maze—then how they would find which direction to go. As they walked they talked about different things. After a while, Allison asked Justin, "What have you enjoyed about our class and how has it helped you?"

Justin was a little taken aback at the talk of finances on a date, but he answered willingly enough. "Well, my mom and my grandpa always stressed paying off credit cards in full. I have more money coming in than going out, and I'm not too flashy with my money—I just basically pay for a car and food, and save up for tuition—though I do have to admit that Professor Christensen's class has helped a lot, with the scholarships and the money management."

"I know what you mean," said Allison. "It's been a huge blessing in *my* life too. I have received two scholarships out of the eleven that I've applied for—plus the Pell Grant."

"Good for you!" Justin remarked.

"That was money I didn't have to earn," she said. "How many scholarships have you applied for?"

"Twenty-one," Justin said.

"Whoa! How'd you apply to so many?" Allison asked.

"I made a system to help me apply faster," he replied.

"Could you teach me later how you did that?"

"Sure. When school started, my dad's company had layoffs, and, because he had to take a pay cut or be laid off, he couldn't pay for my schooling. I was really worried, but now I am getting more money coming to me than if he actually had paid for it—thanks to Professor Christensen's class. What have you learned from the class?"

"My dad taught me to live within my means, but I really like automatic saving and debt prevention. I have also been enjoying the real estate and business concepts.[39] These have really helped toward my goals."

"What's your savings goal?" Justin asked.

"I've always dreamt of going to Beijing. What's your goal?"

---

39 The reader can get the author's books (when available) entitled *Finding College Cash — Housing* and *Finding College Cash — Business* at www.FindingCollegeCash.com

"Buy a property when I graduate, graduate without student loans or credit card debt, and go on a trip to Chichen Itza. I've wanted to go since I was in Mexico," he answered enthusiastically.

"It's so much easier since I started doing my finances automatically," Allison said. "Previously, I didn't have any real hope; Beijing was just a wish, but now I have a plan and it feels so good that I'll go there debt-free."

"I know what you mean," said Justin. "My life is easier when I don't have to worry about paying my bills myself."

They continued talking and Allison said, "I'm working a swing shift at a hotel. I work Monday to Friday. That lets me get my homework done."

"Wait," said Justin. "Every time we've met up for study groups—how could you come if you had a swing shift?"

"My work's really flexible, as long as it's not the holiday season. I can request time off for a study group. Plus I only work four days a week, so I can move my schedule around as long as I give advance notice," Allison explained.

"Gotcha," said Justin. "That's cool. How long have you been doing the hotel job?"

"Well, the hotel is really just for college, since it lets me work on my homework at the same time."

"Yeah, me too!" said Justin. "I work at the computer lab, and that's kind of how *my* job is."

"Oh, really?" said Allison. "That's awesome!"

Justin talked a little bit more about being a lab aide; he really enjoyed doing his homework while getting paid.

Allison agreed, "Yeah, I really enjoy that part of the hotel. That's why I work at the fast-food café too."

"What do you mean?" asked Justin.

"Well," Allison said, "at the end of the day they have leftovers, and the leftovers are offered to the employees at a huge discount. I try to stick to the healthier stuff; things like salads, baked potatoes, soup, and the grilled chicken, or whatever, always come in handy."

Justin nodded in agreement.

"However," Allison added, "I'm going to quit the fast food job soon and change my shift at work; scholarships have helped a lot."

After the maze, they shared some hot cider Justin had brought in a thermos. He drove Allison home.

"See you in class," she said as they hugged briefly in parting.

Chapter 11: Principles and Suggestions

1. Automating your financial life reduces stress and worry—and helps you stay in control. While there are a few pieces, once they are set up, you just need to do minimal maintenance.

2. Be willing to discuss money topics, with your friends and what helps them save money.

Chapter 11: Assignments

1. Complete the "BillPay" exercise in the workbook.

2. Talk with people you trust about what you are doing to pay for college. Ask for ideas on what you can do to pay for college.

Chapter 11: Warnings and What to Avoid

1. The biggest problem with automating your finances is that you will keep delaying it or only set it up part of the way. Please take the time to complete all the steps.

Chapter 12
Final Parts to a Money System

NOTE: This next concept can be dangerous for your financial health if you use it incorrectly. While I do advocate getting a credit card, for reasons I will explain, I advocate this _ONLY IF YOU have the cash in the bank before you buy and you set it up to be automatically paid off in full every month._

Understanding Credit Cards

In class the next week, Professor Christensen began class and said "To begin, let's talk about credit cards because I want you to know how to avoid the pitfalls most college students run into. Credit cards have advantages and disadvantages. Most college students get a credit card and treat it as free money—which is a big mistake. Then they spend the next one to ten years paying it off. I want to help you avoid these problems.

The Negatives of Credit Cards

"Credit cards can hurt your finances and future. Does anyone want to share some negative things that they have seen concerning credit cards?" Professor Christensen asked.

"My dad and mom bought things on credit cards," Maria stated. "They eventually had to declare bankruptcy because they couldn't keep up with the interest and fees."

"My cousin," Allison added, "was going to college and got a credit card that was mailed to him for a T-shirt. The card had a 29% interest rate and the ironic thing was that there was only a five-day grace period. The card advertised that it was a great starter card, but my cousin could barely make a payment on time because of how the card payment cycles behaved."

"Some people in my family have credit cards, and the debt never seems to go away," Tyler said. "They pay money, but never seem to make a dent."

"Do you see the problems here?" Professor Christensen asked. "Credit cards are easy to obtain and merchants make it easy for you to use them in most cases. People get into trouble in one of two ways: One, they get the wrong type of card that has fees, a small grace period, high interest rates, or lack of flexibility in some other way; or two, they don't pay their credit cards off in full every month—they borrow too much from the future. Simply by looking at the terms and conditions of a card, getting free rewards cards, having enough money in the bank, and paying your card off in full each month, you can avoid the major pitfalls of credit cards.

"Credit cards make it extremely easy to buy things, and give you the feeling that 'you can buy now and pay later.' You need to know that when you pay later, you pay more. This is where you must set your own limits and only use the card for pre-determined purchases.

"Do you remember the analogy I shared with you about using a coupon to pay more?" The professor asked. (See chapter 7.)

Several students nodded in agreement.

"Well, this unfortunately, is true for too many people," Professor Christensen responded. "They keep paying and paying and never seem to stop. If you are going to have a credit card, use these rules (he brought them up on the overhead projector):

Credit Card Rules

- Commit to having the money in full before using a credit card.
- Commit to paying the entire balance off every month—automatically, the same day each month (e.g., day 10).
- Commit to logging into your online account every month and review the charges (e.g., day 3).
- Commit to contacting the credit card company immediately if any problem arises from your monthly balance check.
- Commit to using a credit card ONLY for recurring payments (fixed expenses), and large purchases—when you have cash.
- Only get a credit card with a grace period ≥ 20 days.
- NOTE: Interest rates do not matter. Why? You are paying your card off in full and on time every month. **Never pay interest.**

Justin raised his hand and asked, "Why are you suggesting that I log in to my online credit card profile each month?"

"Great question!" Professor Christensen said. "Actually, I recommend that you log into all bank, debit, and credit card accounts each month. Give yourself a monthly financial checkup. You can do nothing wrong, and any of these can be compromised or have fraudulent activity. If you have paid your taxes, shopped at major retailers, or purchased items online in the last few years, you could be the victim of identity theft. Logging in each month allows you to see if something changed. In a moment we will discuss paying your fixed expenses with a credit card."

"I get that, Allison said. "But how can I remember to do this?"

"Set a recurring reminder on your phone or email, and perhaps a reward you may like, such as a small candy bar or fruit for completing the review." Professor Christensen replied. "The point is that you have this review time. Most credit cards have a 60-day dispute time frame. Having your monthly review allows you time to catch problems before your automatic payment kicks in. This way your checking account is also protected from account overcharges.

"Now, if you choose not to use a credit card, you should still have this monthly review. The sooner you can catch a problem with any of your financial accounts, the better off you will be." Professor Christensen smiled and asked, "Are you *scared* yet?"

Many students chuckled.

The Benefits of Using a Good Credit Card

"What good is having a credit card compared to a debit card or just paying cash?" Allison asked.

The professor clicked up another slide. "Credit cards have many advantages—be sure to check terms and conditions, and ask before you sign up. Common benefits are:

- Free merchant fulfillment protection—if your order was different than what you agreed, or the merchant didn't do what they said they would, the credit card company can protect you.
- Free extension of the manufacturer's warranty on many purchases.
- Free-return coverage for 90 days to return some unwanted items.
- Free travel accident insurance.
- Free entertainment services to get concert tickets and other entertainment services (must pay for entertainment purchased).
- Free rental car insurance (up to a limit).
- Free expense tracking, as with a debit card.

In all of these instances, having a credit card can protect you and benefit you in ways that cash and debit cards usually don't. If you use your credit card to only pay your fixed expenses and only use it after you saved the cash, you can avoid the problems most students have. The trick is to pay off your card in full each month.

How to Find a Good Rewards Credit Card

"Good," said the professor. "Now for the rewards credit cards.[40] Generally, avoid card offers that come in the mail or on campus; avoid credit cards that are specific to any one merchant—both the cards in the mail and the merchant cards tend to have the most penalties and highest interest, often with the least amount of flexibility and may hurt your credit.

"Get credit cards that give you more advantage than what it costs for the card. Paying $19 to get a 1%-back card is not that great an idea, as you need to spend $1,900 before you start seeing any profits. *Break-even point = $19/1% = $19/0.01 = $1,900.* Still, *paying* to receive rewards doesn't always benefit you, as the credit card company may change its rewards program, and you would be out the cost of the rewards card, plus, you lose the interest you could have earned on purchases. Paying for a credit card generally makes sense if you are getting high rewards upfront, such as two round-trip plane tickets or something similar. You can find several great free and paid credit cards by going to creditcards.com or www.credit.com/credit-cards. Be sure to read the terms and ensure that rewards are not just *temporary* or *introductory*.

Why Credit Cards Can Be Good for Fixed Expenses

"If you will only spend the total amount of your fixed expenses every month (at least the ones that don't have a fee), you can instantly know if

---

40 The author realizes that getting a good credit card depends on good credit. For more suggestions on improving credit, please see the author's book entitled: *Finding College Cash Housing.*

something changed. If your fixed expenses add up to $137.08 each month (excluding rent and tithing), and when you have your monthly checkup you see $159.53, you will instantly know there was a problem. You then have time to correct the problem before you are billed. You see, having the credit card can act as a buffer; you can just pay one time instead of five to twenty times each month; paying once can be helpful for managing your checking account and high-yield savings accounts because you can know how much to route to each account. Because you automatically pay your credit card off in full each month, you can build good credit."

"Any questions?" Professor Christensen asked.

"My apartment won't accept credit cards without a fee. Is it worth it to get the rewards?" Maria asked.

"Generally, no; don't use your credit card if there will be a transactional fee charged to you. If the merchant doesn't accept credit cards, or if you can't pay automatically without a penalty, then for the majority of cases I would say no, don't use a credit card. If you'd like to automate and the place you need to pay won't accept your credit card without a penalty, I have something better in mind," Professor Christensen said. "But before I introduce that concept, any other questions?"

"Why do I need a grace period of 20 days or more?" Tyler asked.

"The reason," Professor Christensen said, "is that it allows you to set up automatic payments on the same day of the month, and it allows you to have more of a buffer to correct errors if they arise."

"Got it," Tyler replied.

"Why do you suggest we don't use a credit card for daily expenses?" Malcolm asked. "Why not claim the free points?"

"Malcolm," Professor Christensen said with delight, "I think that is a very insightful question. The reason that I am against using a credit card for day-to-day expenses is that it is too easy to exceed your limits. You already can get rewards from a special debit card (either reloadable or configured in relation to your checking account like we discussed). Plus, it is less common to have problems with day-to-day expenses than it is with your large or recurring expenses. Credit cards offer additional layers of protection.

"Let me give an example," Professor Christensen continued. "I once hired a lawyer to do some legal work for me. The lawyer only did part of what he was supposed to do. When I brought this to his attention, he basically ignored me and stopped talking to me. Now if I had paid with cash, check, or debit card, the only recourses I would have had would be to sue him, file a legal complaint with the state bar association, or 'eat' the cost and live with the result. I don't know about you, but taking a lawyer to court or starting a lengthy legal dispute with a lawyer was not something I wanted to do. However, because I used my credit card, I filed a dispute with the credit card company, the credit card legal team pulled the money back from the lawyer while the investigation took place, and suddenly the lawyer who had ignored me wanted to open discussion. We came to agreement and resolution. Now, granted, I did have the money in advance and paid my card in full, but why should I get less than full service for what we had previously agreed?"[41]

That is crazy, Justin thought to himself. *Professor Christensen was sure lucky he didn't have to go to court with a lawyer because he knew how to use a credit card. Using a credit card can do more for me than just build credit or offer rewards; credit cards can protect the consumer with all those benefits he was talking about.*

"However, I caution you," Professor Christen said interrupting Justin's thoughts. "Only use a credit card if you already have the cash before you buy anything on it, do your monthly checkup, and pay it off in full each month. Otherwise, you will get burned. If you don't have the discipline to do these things, *DON'T* sign up for a credit card. Credit cards are not 'free money.'

---

41 This is a real experience of the author. Having the credit card saved me from getting shortchanged by a lawyer.

What to Do If You Are in Credit Card Trouble

"If you ever fail to follow these rules of credit cards, immediately call your credit card company and ask for your card to be frozen, and then work to rapidly pay off the balance. Ask them if you can reduce the interest rate since you have paid off your card in full each month.

"If you ever notice a charge that you did not make," he said, "call your credit card company before 60 days have passed and dispute the charge. This will save you from the hassle of identity theft. Specific to identity theft and fraud, there is a longer time frame for disputing a fraudulent charge, but if you can do this before the end of 60 days it is much easier. Merchant protection must be disputed before the end of 60 days. This is why I suggest you do a monthly checkup.

Rewards Credit Cards

"Credit cards can be a two-edged sword. Let me share an idea that can help you. Did anyone make a trip your diamond goal?" Professor Christensen asked.

Several people raised their hands.

"Great. Let me give you a tip that will greatly help you: Get a rewards credit card that offers you a lot of airline miles up front (say, 30,000 to 50,000 points) if you spend a few thousand dollars in two to three months' time. Pay tuition with this credit card, and earn a free trip. Check with your 529 savings plan and see if you can get reimbursed for a qualified expense; that is, if you can reimburse yourself for paying for tuition, thereby saving money on state taxes and free gains. If so, pay the card off in full from money in your 529 savings plan, or if not from your checking account. By doing this, you just earned a free trip or more.

"You may want to consider getting two credit cards: a free rewards card that you will use for your fixed expenses, and a paid credit card for large purchases like tuition that offers an enormous amount of points upfront."

"Wait!" Tyler exclaimed, "Are you saying we can get a free trip just for paying tuition?"

"You do need to have the cash up front, and check the terms of the credit card," Professor Christensen replied.

Justin realized that he could get a lot of points just for paying for tuition. *Chichen Itza might be closer than I think.*

"Great!" Malcolm blurted out. "Now you tell me, after I've already paid this semester's tuition."

"If you have already paid this semester's tuition, keep it in mind for next semester, or see if the tuition office will let you pay with your credit card now and get a check back," the professor said. "*HOWEVER,* before you get too excited, please remember that this is only to be used if you have the cash up front and follow the rules about using a credit card."

"Excuse me, professor," Allison said, "you mentioned that some merchants won't accept credit cards without a fee. What should I do about fixed expenses that won't accept credit cards?"

"True, some places have a fee," Professor Christensen said, "but this is where Bill Pay comes in."

"Got it," Allison responded.

Plinko

Professor Christensen asked the class, "Has anyone seen the TV game show *The Price is Right?*"

"Who hasn't?" Malcolm asked.

"Has anyone seen the game Plinko?" Professor Christensen continued. A few students had. "Can anyone explain the game?"

Tyler made the attempt: "Plinko is a game where contestants drop a circular disk on a vertical board that has pegs on it. The disk will fall either to the left or right when it hits the peg. At the bottom, the disk goes into different slots that offer different levels of prizes. The contestants try to start the disk on the right track so it hits the biggest prize as it falls."

"Very well said!" Professor Christensen commented. "I want to show you a system to place your money automatically into the right slot—so you don't have to think about it."

"How is that going to work?" Maria asked, curiously.

"The good news," Professor Christensen said, "is that we have already set up many of the parts needed. By now most of you have found your *bubblegum-diamond-thieves*, allocated paychecks to a high-yield account, adjusted tax exemptions, added income sources to your life, and decided on at least one fun goal to work towards.

Cash Flow Hierarchy

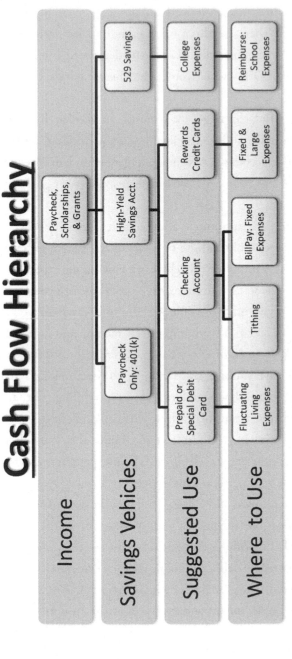

Cash Flow Hierarchy

Income — Paycheck, Scholarships, & Grants

Savings Vehicles — Paycheck Only: 401(k) | High-Yield Savings Acct. | 529 Savings

Suggested Use — Prepaid or Special Debit Card | Checking Account | Rewards Credit Cards | College Expenses

Where to Use — Fluctuating Living Expenses | Tithing | BillPay: Fixed Expenses | Fixed & Large Expenses | Reimburse: School Expenses

Note 1: Use your *Prepaid/Special* debit card for daily expenses. Avoid carrying a credit card.

Note 2: You should purchase large expenses (e.g. tuition) with credit card to get rewards—but only if there's NO fee for using a credit card. Pay the card off monthly in full automatically.

Note 3: Reimburse yourself from a 529 Savings Plan for paying school expenses (see your 529 Savings Plan details). School expenses include tuition, class fees, books, and housing (limited).

"The point is that money automatically goes where it needs to be. You determine in advance how much you need and put it there. You can make adjustments if needed. There are three more parts that we need to talk about: Bill Pay, a rewards credit card, and a prepaid debit card. But for now, let's focus on the flow of cash—when you get it, where it goes and how to do this automatically."

"Paychecks and scholarships go to a money market or high-yield savings account, a 529 Savings Plan, and if your work provides it, a 401(k) plan. The money market account holds your emergency fund, or a freedom continuation plan, savings for your future expenses, and your goals-and-dreams money.

"Money flows from one account to another, automatically," Professor Christensen said, "but you only will use one part of the system for every-day expenses—and that is your prepaid debit card. Fluctuating expenses get paid with your prepaid debit card; fixed expenses get paid with your credit card (if you choose to have one) and Bill Pay. You only carry the prepaid debit card. This will prevent you from impulsively buying, and it prevents you from having to keep track of every penny, which a lot of budgeting systems and software have you do. This is similar to the envelope system that many people use, but rather than having to keep refilling your envelopes each month, it happens automatically—plus you don't have to carry wads of cash around with you. You just have to commit that you will live only on the money on your prepaid debit card. If you spend too much on junk, you had better be willing to eat a lot of rice.

"Use a rewards credit card and Bill Pay and pay the credit card off in full every month. This is one of the key parts; you use a rewards card for fixed expenses (amounts that don't change each month—cell phone, rent, insurance, etc.), and a prepaid debit card for fluctuating expenses (food, gas, fun, entertainment, etc.). The prepaid debit card I will talk about in more depth a little bit later, but let me explain the use of credit cards first."

Step-By-Step Process

"Is there a step-by-step method?" Tyler asked.

"I'm glad you asked," Professor Christensen said as he advanced the slide and announced: "Process for a paycheck. This will be a slight repeat, but I want to make sure that you get this. It is crucial for you to understand this plan."

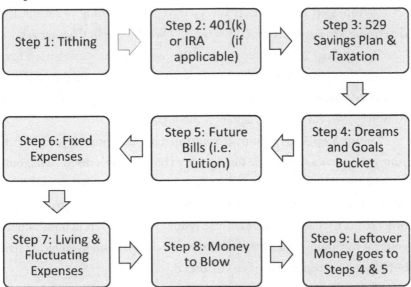

"The key here is to have money flow automatically; set it up once and you are done worrying about where your money is going," the professor said. "Think of each step as a slice of your total income; by the time it gets to less important things, the important ones have already been taken care of. The point is not to waste your money on useless things, but to get what you really want."

"Do we pay off each of those steps in the graphic completely?" Allison asked.

"Each step gets a slice of your total income—either a percentage or a fixed amount. I put the items in order of payment priority. Some items like your future tuition you may not be able to pay off from one paycheck, but saving up for it over time helps lots."

"'Kay. That helps clarify things for me," Allison said. Professor Christensen returned to the graphic to explain.

Easy Money System Setup

"It really only takes a few steps to set up, and a few steps to implement each month," Professor Christensen said.

"**Setup-Step 1:** Set a really fun goal to get something you want, and determine a basic plan to work toward it." [We did this in Chapter 7.]

"**Setup-Step 2:** Sort your present expenses into three categories: fixed expenses (expenses that don't change, such as rent), fluctuating expenses (ones that change, such as your grocery bill), and future bills (for example, tuition)." [We did this in Chapters 7 and 8.]

"**Setup-Step 3:** Determine if your expenses are bringing you closer to your goals (diamonds) or are unnecessary (bubblegum); decide what bubblegum you do want to keep (e.g., $10 per month to be with friends), but keep it minimal. Eliminate expenses that you would be willing to give up in order to get to your goal (for example, reduce fast food, buy in bulk, and sell your car to eliminate gasoline and insurance costs). Would you rather have bubblegum or diamonds?" [See Chapter 8.]

"**Setup-Step 4:** Find out if your fixed expenses can be paid by a credit card *without a fee* and billed automatically. If they can't, inquire about their address to mail a payment to so you can use Bill Pay (or other online bill payment service from your bank; see Setup-Step 6)."

"**Setup-Step 5:** Open a money market account or high-yield savings account (link to checking account(s) opened in Setup-Steps 6 and 7). Get the routing and account numbers of this account.

"**Setup-Step 6:** Open a checking account with free Bill Pay, preferably at the same bank as the account opened in Setup-Step 5.

"**Setup-Step 7:** Get a prepaid debit card, or get another checking account and ask the bank in writing to deny the charges if it exceeds the money in the account." [We did this in Chapters 10 and 11.]

"**Setup-Step 8 (optional)**: Open a 529 Education Savings Plan if you have a few years before graduating college and/or if your state offers a state income tax credit. Pull your educational expenses from this account.

"**Setup-Step 9**: Allocate your money among your fixed, fluctuating, and future expenses, and determine when it should arrive in your accounts. Set up automatic recurring transfers once or twice a month from the high-yield savings account to your checking account. From the checking account, transfer money to your prepaid or special debit card. In the same checking account keep the money for Bill Pay and your credit card bill. (You should know the exact amount of money for your fixed expenses.)

"After setting things up, your money will go automatically to the designated place:

"**Step 1**: Pay your tithing first (you decide whether to tithe before or after tax).

"**Step 2**: Allocate an amount to go to your 401(k) or IRA before the government takes *its* bite, or use a Roth IRA. Even if it is $20 per month, this will allow you to get any matching that your employer offers, and will help get you in the habit of saving."

"What if my job doesn't offer a 401(k) plan?" Maria asked.

"Consider participating in a Roth IRA—which takes funds after tax, but grows tax-free," Professor Christensen said.

"**Step 3** (multiple sub-steps):

Allocate your W4 to have the correct amount of exemptions to prevent being over-taxed—speak to your accountant and HR representative.

- (This sub-step fits in both steps 3 and 5.) Decide to open a 529 Savings Plan. Use it to save money for school expenses. The Utah ESP is a great resource.
- Open a money market account that pays about one percent, such as with Ally or Barclay's. Have your money and/or paycheck go automatically into your money market or high-yield

savings account—without going to the bank to cash your check—using direct deposit with your employer."

o   Alternatively, if your employer doesn't allow direct deposit, inquire if your bank has a money market account and an app for your smartphone that deposits checks with pictures.

"**Step 4:** Start living your dreams. What do you really want? Find out how much it costs, and then set aside money until you get it (something like $50 per month)."

"Wouldn't it be better to just buy what you want and pay it off so you can enjoy it longer?" Tyler asked.

"Great question," Professor Christensen said. "What's something you want?"

"I want a new laptop—in fact, I need one for school, and it'd be nice to have to watch movies with."

"A new laptop costs about $350 to $2,500 depending on type and style. If you were to purchase it using a credit card, even if you paid it off in five years, you would spend 1.4 to 1.9 times as much on your computer. What could Tyler do while he is saving up to buy a computer?" Professor Christensen asked the class.

"Borrow a friend's."

"Use the campus computers."

"If you don't need to have a brand new one, there are plenty of used computers for under $100 available on ebay.com or amazon.com."

"Great ideas!" Professor Christensen said. "If you absolutely must have a new one, why not save up and wait until the Friday through Monday right after Thanksgiving? Stores cut prices on many items by 20–80% and you can get a new computer for hundreds less. But even more important than getting a deal, you'll have purchased it debt-free by saving up. There'll be no dragon looming over your life because you haven't paid your bills. You won't have constant worry and you won't end up being 'a day late and a dollar short.'"

"I had never thought of those ideas," Tyler said.

"Another problem with buying before you have the money is: when do you stop? When do you stop buying things before you have the money? If you buy a laptop, it could become a habit and then soon you might buy clothing, MP3s, shoes, and even groceries on credit. The only way to stop this pattern is to decide not to do use it.

"**Step 5**: Similar to Step 4, if you know you have big expenses coming, such as next semester's tuition, save up for it now. I recommend that you use a 529 Education Savings Plan to contribute money automatically. This may also save you money on state income taxes while allowing your money to grow tax-free. You may be able to get a credit from some states.

"If you happen to have scholarships available to you, I recommend that you check with the school's tuition office about what happens if you overpay tuition. Many times, if there's a surplus of funds, you can have the money returned to you. For example, if you have a scholarship that covers tuition, and you were to pay with a 529 Savings plan, you would get to keep the money from the scholarship and get the tax and savings benefits from using your 529 savings plan—a double win."

Justin smiled at this idea because he had already had gotten refunded money from the tuition office—several times over.

"Other bills can and should be saved up for in advance. This makes your financial life cheaper and easier by not having to pay for items over and over again by paying interest and penalties. Save for your bills before purchase.

"Next, let's automate where your paycheck goes. Make your life simple. Set things up once and you're done. You review periodically, but mostly you just set up automatic payments and let your bills get taken care of automatically. That way, you'll *never have* a late payment or interest. Automate your financial life. The more manual action people's systems require, the more unlikely it is that they'll have financial success. This is why I suggest automating your payments."

"That'd be nice," Malcolm said.

Professor Christensen smiled.

"**Step 6:** Add up all your fixed expenses—things like cell phone, rent, insurance, and other expenses that don't change from month to month, or year to year, and pay them all with a designated rewards credit card used only for your fixed expenses.

"**Step 7:** Get a prepaid debit or special debit card from your bank that will only allow you to use up to a specified amount. You can find these cards at creditcards.com or www.credit.com/credit-cards. Decide on what you need for fluctuating expenses: food, gas, and fun. Use only this card. Leave your other cards at home. You can spend your money on whatever you want, but know this: if you use your money for the month on a lot of worthless junk, you will be eating ramen noodles for the rest of the month.

"**Step 8:** Go blow some money. If you have already allocated your money and paid your expenses, go have some fun using your prepaid debit card. Decide in advance how much you will spend each month on everyday expenses; if there is money left on the prepaid debit card, you get to use it. This is a reward for managing your money well.

"**Step 9:** If you want your future goal more than blowing money, put the remainder of the money back towards steps 4 and 5."

Maria raised her hand. "That seems a whole lot easier than worrying about paying my bills like my rent and phone each month. I mean, I think that I will enjoy having bills paid automatically."

"I am glad you think so," Professor Christensen said. "This is your assignment," as he advanced the slide. He read aloud:

Chapter 12: Principles and Suggestions

1. Automate everything financial in your life. Set up your paycheck and scholarships to be deposited directly into your bank account.

2. Get a free rewards credit card if you don't already have one. See if you can

get one by going to creditcards.com or www.credit.com/credit-cards and applying online. Use this card exclusively for fixed payments.

a. **<u>PAY THE CARD OFF IN FULL</u>** each month, automatically, by contacting the credit card company and linking it to your checking account.

b. You may want to get a second high rewards credit card that offers you a lot of points, cash, or a trip upfront for spending $1,000–3,000. Get and use this high rewards card near the start of a semester to get a huge reward for paying tuition.

3. For individuals and companies that either do not accept credit cards or charge a fee to use them, use Bill Pay to send them a recurring check from your checking account.

4. Get a reloadable, prepaid debit card from your bank or site like nerdwallet.com that only allows you to spend what you fund on the card (this works mostly like cash, except you will not accidentally exceed a limit and get charged a fee, as you would with a debit card).

5. Find what you can eliminate from your expenses:

a. Sell your car and using a bike and public transportation

b. Use coupons and promotion codes (i.e. Groupon)

c. Use the library instead of the movie theater

d. Reduce eating out

e. Getting a job closer to where you live

f. Buy in bulk (e.g. oatmeal, pasta, toilet paper, etc.)

g. Change apartments to be closer to school and work

Chapter 12: Assignments

1. Decide if you are willing to abide by the rules for credit cards listed in this chapter.

    a.   If so, go to sites like www.credit.com/credit-cards creditcards.com and inquire about a good rewards credit card to help you get to your goal.

        • DON'T get a credit card that comes in the mail to students or one you see advertised on campuses.

    b.   If you aren't willing to follow the credit card rules, set your fixed expenses up with Bill Pay from your bank.

2. Complete the exercises on credit cards in the workbook.

3. Review the Cash Flow Hierarchy and Step-By-Step Process; make your finances emulate these models.

Chapter 12: Warnings and What to Avoid

1. Never cash a check at a check cashing location—they charge three to nine percent of your check. Use your bank, or the check issuer's bank, instead.

2. Get rewards credit cards to pay off fixed and fluctuating expenses. WARNINGS:

    a.   Link the credit cards to your checking account or you won't be able to automatically pay the balance (call the credit card company for directions).

    b.   Make sure that the credit card allows at least 20 days for a grace period.

    c.   Pay the credit card off in full on the same day each month; if you don't, you will be charged interest and penalties, and may lose your rewards.

    d.   Get a rewards credit card for fixed expenses, and a prepaid debit card for your monthly expenses. Only carry the prepaid card with you.

3. Avoid paying for your goals and dreams until you have the cash. Things get cheaper when you save, but more expensive when you buy on credit.

4. While you are encouraged to "blow" some of your money, don't overdo it. Plan in advance what you can realistically afford, without sacrificing your goals, dreams, and other expenses, and then spend only that amount. Find cheaper ways to do the same thing. Instead of going to a newly released movie, wait three months, rent it for under two dollars and have a party at a neighbor's apartment.

5. Avoid getting credit cards from department stores and mail promotions. Most of the time these have really steep penalties, interest, and other charges. Additionally, they don't really help build your credit.

"Any questions?" the professor asked when he had finished reading the slide. No hands went up. "Well, no class until next week. In the meantime, apply for another scholarship and automate your financial life."

The bell rang, and Justin was amazed that Professor Christensen could both teach them how to spend purposefully *and* be so good at timing his lecture to end just before the bell.

Chapter 13
Automatic Money Success

At this point, Justin had gathered information about his finances and he was ready to start automating payments. At work he looked at his credit card bill and spotted a couple of things he had not noticed before: The company charged him an annual fee of $23 and offered him 1.2% rewards.

Let me see... Justin opened the calculator on the computer and typed in the break-even equation: Break-even equation = $23.00/0.012 = $1,916.67. *I have to spend almost $2,000 before I can even start making a profit!!! That's ridiculous.* He navigated his browser to creditcards.com and credit.com/credit-cards and did quick credit card searches. He soon found that there were many free rewards cards available. *Miles, points, or cash: which do I want?* Justin jotted some cards down, along with a few of the other offers, and then got ready to leave the lab.

When Erin arrived, Justin grabbed his stuff, and left. On his way back to his car, Justin pulled out his credit card, dialed the number on the back of it, and asked to speak to a manager.

"Let me check to see if one is available," the representative said. After a moment, she said, "I can transfer you to Mr. Sullivan."[42]

"Thanks," said Justin, relieved at his request not being denied.

After a few minutes, a voice on the other end said, "Hello, this is Peter Sullivan. Whom do I have the pleasure of speaking with?"

---

42 Receptionists have the power to say no but rarely have the power to say yes. Speak to a supervisor.

Justin gave his name and verified his account information.

"What can I do for you?" Mr. Sullivan asked.

"I was wondering if I could be switched to a free rewards credit card," Justin responded. "I have the paid version of the card, but I would like to have the free version."

"The free version has half the rewards points," Mr. Sullivan said.

"I know," said Justin, "but right now I have to spend over $1,900 before I see a penny of rewards anyway. Will I lose any points I *have* acquired?"

"There is no loss of accrued points if you convert to the free card,"[43] Mr. Sullivan said, in a tone that conveyed he knew what Justin was referring to.

"Great, may I keep the same credit card number?"

"We will send you a new card," Mr. Sullivan replied.

"Let me give you my updated address." Justin provided his new address and then confirmed the conversion of the card. He thanked Mr. Sullivan for his time and ended the call.

After hanging up the phone, Justin was amazed that it had been so easy. *Mr. Sullivan sounded as if he knew that people must spend thousands of dollars before they see any rewards.* Justin smiled to himself as he walked home. He was now more aware of the game that credit card companies played. He wondered about how much money people lost on credit cards that have a much higher annual fee than his did—just to get a 'reward.'

Getting a Better Credit Card

Justin was on a roll. *I wonder if I can get a bigger rewards card for free.* He decided to return to creditcards.com, and there he found one that offered 50,000 airline miles, or two domestic round-trip tickets. He applied for a credit card and was approved for a small credit limit. The card would arrive in about ten days.

---

43 Converting with the same company may allow you to keep your accrued points. If the rewards points are not preserved with a conversion, redeem what you can, and then convert the old credit card to a new free rewards card. For credit building purposes, it is a good idea to have one credit card without an annual fee that you keep for years.

Recap—Start of Dreams

The next day Justin went on a run with Paul. Justin told his story.

"Tell me again what the credit card guy did when you pointed out how much you had to spend before points helped," Paul requested.

"He was just kind of dumbfounded and didn't really have a rebuttal—it was kind of like he knew that many paid credit cards like that one are a waste of money," Justin replied, repeating what Mr. Sullivan had said.

Paul laughed in disbelief. "Man, that is just crazy. You have even got me thinking of how to reduce my wasted money. You really lucked out with this class."

"I know. It really has been a gift from God. But get this … I checked at creditcards.com and I can get a rewards credit card that offers enough points for two round-trip plane tickets to most places in North America and either a rental car or one night at a mid-level hotel. The only catch is that I have to spend $2,000 in two months. With tuition coming up next semester, that'll be easy—"

"Wait," interjected Paul, "credit cards are the worst way to pay for school because they have such high rates. Why would your professor tell you to use one of those?"

"I already have the cash for next semester, so I would pay it off in full before any interest accrued."

"So where are you going to go? Wait, let me guess … El Paso, Texas." Paul said with a smile. Justin frowned.

"Detroit?" Paul asked wryly.

"I was thinking of using all my points to take me to …"

"Chichen Itza," Paul and Justin said in unison.

"I knew that," Paul said with a smile. "You've been talking about it since we were in Mexico. I just thought that it was kind of a dream, but now I can see that you have a plan, and I believe you will get there."

"Thanks," Justin smiled. "You should come with me. Let's go next July."

"I would love to; it's just that Anna and I are getting closer and you might be coming to my wedding at about that time."

"Did you propose?" Justin asked curiously.

"Not yet, but perhaps soon," Paul said with a smile.

Linking Credit Cards with Checking Accounts

True to the company's word, Justin's new rewards credit card arrived in a few days. He called to confirm receiving the card and got it activated. He then asked to speak with a representative.

"Good morning, Mr. Murray," the representative said. "What can I do for you?"

"Well," said Justin, "I was wondering how I would link my new credit card to my checking account and set it up so the card will automatically pull money from my checking account each month and pay off the entire balance in full."

"That's a great question," the representative said. "You will need to have your account number and routing number and either provide them over the phone or log into your account online and do it there."

"I think that I'd like to complete it online," Justin said.

The representative told Justin how to link his checking account to the credit card and then confirm the linked accounts. He also told Justin how to set up the billing so that the card balance would be automatically paid each month, allowing Justin to pick the day he wanted the money to be pulled from his checking account.

When Justin had a moment to get online, he linked his checking account and credit card and setup the credit card to pay off in full on the 10th day of each month. He noticed a section called "E-mail Alerts," and set up both an alert to go to his email and a text reminder to go to his cell phone so that he'd be sure to have deposited enough money in his account in time.

Automate Payments with Credit Cards and Bill Pay

On *his* free credit card, Justin was only going to put his fixed expenses that allowed credit card payments with no fees. He'd use Bill Pay for other fixed expenses.

Justin decided to put everything he could onto automatic bill paying by using both the Bill Pay service and his rewards credit card to pay his fixed bills. He figured that since rent was due on the 5th of the month, he would pay every other fixed expense on the 15th of each month—this allowed him to break up his expenses.

Justin logged onto his accounts for his cell phone, auto insurance, and internet service (the internet provider had unique logon accounts for each roommate), and wrote down his account numbers and the addresses to send payments to, and also checked to see if they allowed payment by credit card. He entered the pertinent information into MS Excel, since some of the websites logged him off. He already knew where to send his rent, and now he could pay all of his fixed expenses using Bill Pay or his rewards credit card. He then went to each account and changed his billing methods.

His car insurance company already allowed him to use his credit card directly, so he figured, *Well, why don't I make that payment due on the 1st of each month and have it automatically bill my credit card, then I can pay my credit card off on the 5th of the month—the same day rent is due, just to remind myself to pay all my bills on that day?* He went to the website of his auto insurer and called a representative to change his billing date to the first of the month and have his credit card billed directly. The attendant was happy to oblige and make these changes. In passing, Justin mentioned the fact that he was a student at a university.

"Oh, you started school? That's wonderful!" remarked the agent. "Did you happen to know we offer a student discount on our car insurance?"

"No, I didn't," said Justin.

"Well, we do. All you have to do is maintain at least a 'B' average in your classes, and we will consider you to be a good student. At present, do you have that?"

Justin thought about his classes and the grades he'd received. He was pretty sure he had well over a 'B' average. In fact, it was closer to the 'A' range. He mentioned that to the attendant.

She said, "Great! Why don't we apply this discount?"

Justin was very grateful. Now that he had set up his auto insurance to draft on the first day of the month to his credit card with no annual fee and offered rewards, Justin then followed suit with his internet provider and his cell phone.

After putting those bills on his credit card, and setting up the credit card to be paid off in full each month, Justin decided to pay his rent by electronic Bill Pay. He logged onto his checking account, searched, and arranged for a check to arrive by the first day of each month, even though it wasn't due until the fifth day. He wanted to be cautious, in case major holidays or anything else prevented the mail from being delivered exactly by the 5th.

Fluctuating Expenses—Get a Prepaid Debit Card

Justin was relieved that he no longer needed to worry about being late with his bill payments; they were all taken care of automatically. He wrote his one-page paper, describing what he had done to automate his financial life. In the paper, he explained that he was earning about 1% interest from a money market account, saving about 2% making purchases he would have made anyway, saving 5% by contributing to his 529 savings plan and not having to pay state income tax on however much those contributions grew, and preventing spending too much by using a his special debit card—all set up to process automatically. He was now free to spend $265 in the manner he deemed best—in addition to saving for his dreams of going to Chichen Itza and buying a property and providing for future goals and ambitions with his 529 Savings Plan and his money market account. Life had just gotten better financially, that's for sure.

Justin submitted his paper on the class website and then went looking for a scholarship to which he could submit his essay. He went to fastweb.com and found a scholarship easily. *More free money, here I come!*

Chapter 13: Principles and Suggestions

1. Automate your paycheck going to a money market account using direct deposit.

    a.   Ensure that you follow the instructions for listing exemptions on your W-2, W-4, and other tax forms. Check with your employer or HR department about increasing your exemptions.

2. Pay your fixed expenses with a specific rewards credit card and Bill Pay.

    a.   Pay your credit card balance off in full each month by linking your credit card and primary checking account.

    b.   Don't carry any credit card with you. Keep it separate from your regular purchases by storing it in a secure place.

3. Pay your fluctuating expenses on a prepaid debit card from your bank.

4. Link your money market account, checking account, and credit cards so that your paycheck goes into the money market, then to the checking account, then to pay your bills and credit cards.

5. Ask your employer about tuition reimbursement, scholarships, and 401(k) plans. Apply as directed.

6. Establish a 529 Education Savings Plan. Contribute monthly, and save up for tuition, books, and housing (you may also get a tax break as you save).

7. Each month withdraw the amount you need for fluctuating expenses and automatically have this deposited to your prepaid debit card.

Chapter 13: Warnings and What to Avoid

1. Don't pay for a rewards credit card unless you really get high rewards. It makes no sense to spend $20 per year at 1% return; you would need to spend $2,000 before you even began making a profit. There are lots of free rewards credit cards.

2. Banks will charge you if you use a debit or credit card and go over your balance; this is why it is recommended to use a prepaid debit card that will deny charges if there is not enough money in the account to avoid bank fees.

3. You may need to transfer the money for some expenses (like rent) from your money market account into your checking account on an earlier date than you use for your credit cards and other bills. Try to add up the totals you need and then transfer them to your checking account in a grouped amount (e.g., $20 for laundry, $100 for food, $40 for cell phone = $160; withdraw $160 one time instead of making three withdrawals).

4. Even though things happen automatically, it is still a good idea to review every account at least monthly. This will help you keep yourself in check and avoid errors. You may want to have a password-protected spreadsheet that stores passwords/logins.

Chapter 14
Consequences of Debt

Justin was running low on groceries; it was time to go to the store. After work, he stopped by the store. At the checkout aisle, he saw his cousin Dave. Dave was buying some snacks from the checkout aisle racks. "Hey, Justin! How's college life treating you?"

"Pretty good," Justin said. "I started dating this girl I met in one of my classes."

"Is she cute?" Dave asked.

"Oh, yeah," Justin said with emphasis.

"Well, you should invite her over to our house for dinner. We'd love to meet her."

They talked for a few more minutes. Justin decided it would be fun to see Dave and Susan again, so they decided on Saturday. They set up the time and agreed to meet up.

Saturday came and Justin drove Allison (who had happily agreed to come to dinner) over to meet his cousin and his family. While they were eating, Dave turned to Allison and asked "Justin told me that you two met in a class. What class was it?"

"We met in a personal finance class taught by a visiting professor," Allison explained.

"Wow. No offense—sounds kind of boring. I thought it'd be tennis or ballroom dance or some fun class," Dave said with a smile.

Allison laughed, "Well, I thought the class would be boring

too, but it's been really helpful. We've been learning about scholarships, managing finances, and something I really liked that he calls *bubblegum-diamond-thieves.*"

"What's a bubblegum diamond thief?" Susan asked.

"A bubblegum-diamond-thief is what robs you of your money. You know, the type of stuff that is just quick purchases—maybe two dollars here or 75 cents there, or reoccurring purchases you don't want or use. Those impulse purchases prevent you from having what you really want, and at the end of the month you wonder where all your money went." Allison's enthusiasm showed clearly.

"No kidding," said Dave said with a smile. "What did your professor say to do to stop this thief?"

"He taught us to set a big goal that's really important to us, and then determine what we are willing to sacrifice to achieve it," Allison began.

Justin noticed Susan's lower lip was starting to tremble.

"Sacrifice doesn't mean that we stop having fun," Allison continued, "It just means we do things differently—like waiting to borrow or rent a movie instead of going to see the movie in theaters or making lunch instead of buying fast food, and finding expenses we don't need, like paying interest on credit cards."

"Did your professor say to get rid of all credit cards?" Dave asked.

"Well, no," Allison responded. "He actually told us to get a credit card that offers good rewards, not one of those cards that come in the mail. He also said to pay our bills in full and on time—automatically, so we don't have to worry about them, and then get a prepaid debit card to use for day-to-day purchases. That way we'd never get a late notice, overspend our money, or get hit with an overcharge fee. The money comes into a savings account, and then some goes to goals, future bills, fixed expenses, and a prepaid debit card. This has saved me a lot of worry about money."

Compounded Bad Decisions—How Debt Really Feels

With the mention of 'money worries,' Susan couldn't hold it in any longer and the tears started flowing.

"Did I say something to offend you?" Allison asked, worried that she had said something impolite.

"All we ever do is worry about money," Susan sobbed. Dave put his hand on her shoulder.

"It'll be all right, honey," Dave said. "We'll make it work."

"No, we won't! You are always working, and we never seem to catch up," Susan exclaimed through her tears.

"We didn't mean to upset you," Justin said with compassion; he remembered seeing the overdue notice when he stayed here before.

"It's not your fault, it's ours," Susan said.

"Honey," Dave began.

"No, they should know what it's like on the other side—so they never make the same mistakes we made," Susan retorted, sounding resolute through her tears. Without waiting she continued.

"We both got credit cards when we were in college. I got a stupid water bottle, which I lost within a few weeks, for getting a credit card. It seemed so exciting while I was on campus to get that card. I would go to restaurants with my friends, buy a new outfit, and buy junk that I can't even remember now. I thought that I'd pay it off later, and boy have we paid for it later.

"Dave had the same problems with money as I did. When we were engaged, we just thought that once we graduated, we'd get better jobs and pay off all our debts, credit cards, and student loans, but it didn't happen that way." She took a breath between her sobs.

"We found we could spend more because we were earning more. We bought a bigger house than we needed. We bought a new car because it was just $788 per month. We never realized we'd end up paying over $35,000 for a car that was worth $23,000. But pretty soon, it became hard to keep up with it all. Do you know what it's like having $43,000 in credit card debt, $11,000 left on a car payment, student loans, and a mortgage? It's horrible and depressing; our paychecks are gone by mid-month. The interest alone…it should be criminal to charge anything over 20 percent."

"Honey, I can just put more hours into my job. Could we talk about this later, I mean it's really not that bad," Dave said, noticeably embarrassed.

"Put more hours into your job?! You're already working sixty hours a week. We don't have money and you're gone so much, and we can't afford to even consider having a baby because we can't control our expenses. It *is* that bad. I looked at our bills and credit card statements today. When you go to the store, you come home with junk food and you tell me 'It's no big deal.' We have to pay for things over and over because we never learned to manage money. We keep paying for it later and later. The more we do that, the harder it becomes…and in the end, we have a bunch of worthless junk."

Susan sobbed bitterly. There was a heavy uneasiness in the room. "As you can tell, we have been kind of struggling," Dave said remorsefully.

"Everyone makes mistakes," Justin said. "I could drop off a copy of the notes from the class about managing expenses."

"A government-sponsored debt counselor might be able to help," Allison said.

Dave nodded absently. His attention was on comforting his wife.

Justin turned to Allison and said, "We should go."

Allison nodded.

"Dave, you and Susan can keep the salad and the potatoes," Justin said, wanting to help, but it clearly only made Dave feel worse to receive free food from a college student.

Dave gave a half-smile and nodded.

"I'll drop the notes by later," Justin quickly added.

Justin and Allison said their goodbyes and left. In the car, there was still a heavy feeling. Dave and Susan's dilemma was on both of their minds. Allison was the first to break the silence:

"Sorry about your cousin and his wife," Allison said carefully.

"Me too," Justin replied. "I never realized that they were hurting so much because of money. I now understand why Professor Christensen is so adamant about staying out of debt. It really does crush you."

"I never want to get into debt for things that don't increase in value," Allison said. "I'm so glad Professor Christensen warned us about avoiding debt by watching our *bubblegum-diamond-thieves*."

Chapter 14: Principles and Suggestions

1. Match ads where you can at stores. You can save a lot of money.

2. Be willing to share good ideas, books, and resources with others.

3. Learn to pay for things you can afford; if you wait to pay until later, later usually comes with a higher price tag.

Chapter 14: Assignments

1. Complete the section in the workbook on "Understanding Debt."

2. Make a plan so that you do <u>NOT</u> end up like the characters in this chapter. Make the decision to avoid debt, except for a modest home when you have enough for the down payment.

Chapter 14: Warnings and What to Avoid

1. You can avoid the emotional and financial consequences of debt by watching your bubblegum-diamond-thieves and living within your means.

2. Stay away from debt consolidation companies. These types of companies tend to be dishonest.

3. Being in debt really takes the life out of you. Avoid being in debt for things that depreciate. Pay off your bills in full.

Chapter 15
Keep out of Financial Trouble

During the next class, Professor Christensen said that he wanted to talk about something very important. "Let's talk about expenses."

The True Cost of Debt

"I hope that, with all the time I've spent teaching you about applying for scholarships and minimizing your expenses, you've done that, but in case you haven't, we're going to talk about that right now. I know that we covered some of this before, but I think it's important to bring it up again. One financial blogger who accrued massive amounts of credit card debt bemoaned that she'd spent money on things she didn't need, and then didn't have money when she actually did need it. Another blogger said that the time that was wasted prevented her from taking other opportunities because of the debt that was accumulated.[44] Isn't that sad to hear?

"First and foremost, establish some type of budgeting or accounting system. You need to pay off your credit card in full—every month. If you make large purchases (paying for tuition, for example), rather than just putting it on the credit card and working to pay off the credit card, do it in reverse. Have enough cash in your account to pay off the entire balance, and then try to find a good rewards card and get some money back. But no matter what else you do, pay off your credit card debt in full every month.

---

44 'Emma'. "Mistakes Made with Money." CNN.com Blogs. Accessed August 9, 2017. http://cnnstudentnews.blogs.cnn.com/2010/04/22/mistakes-made-with-money/.

This will allow you to avoid late charges, interest, and penalties, and it will allow you to improve your credit. I can't stress this enough. There are so many Americans who are maxing out their credit cards, and it's just, figuratively speaking, eating them alive."

Professor Christensen asked if anyone would be willing to read something aloud. Tyler said he would, and accepting a paper, read:

> *Debt is slavery. Debt is a thief. Debt steals our todays with worry and concern and robs our hope for tomorrows. People spend money that they haven't yet earned, on the assumption that they will pay out their tomorrows by purchasing on credit; however, they pay for it over and over again. Debt is a dragon that eats people's lives. People are working over and over again for the same items…"*

After Tyler read the quote, Professor Christensen asked: "Do you think that this is true about debt? Why or why not?"

Justin knew this wasn't the setting, but he couldn't help thinking of Dave and Susan and what had happened at their house—when Susan had cried over their finances. *Debt really is a dragon that eats people,* Justin thought to himself. Other students started answering the professor's question.

"Well, if you don't have a car to go to work, wouldn't getting a car help you make more money and be good reason for debt?" Maria inquired.

"I work off campus," Tyler responded, "and obviously I have to pay for gas and insurance for my car—plus the car payment. I thought I needed a car, but it's costing me money. I have my job, and I have some freedom, but I didn't realize what the freedom was costing me. I started thinking after Professor Christensen's lesson on managing expenses that I was spending about half of my paycheck just to have the car. I wish I'd gotten a closer job so I didn't need to commute, or at least not bought my car on credit. I am a slave to my car, instead of having complete freedom."

"Wait, *dude*—" Malcolm interjected, "are you serious?! How do you ever expect to get a date if you can't even show the ladies that you can afford to take care of yourself?"

"I hadn't thought of that," Tyler said.

"Well, some of us 'ladies,'" Allison said, directing a mild glare at Malcolm, "care more about who you are as a person than your car. Let me put it this way: what if your 'lady' marries you for your nice car; when will it stop? Getting a more expensive house than you can afford? Buying a luxury diamond and 18 karat gold necklace? Taking expensive vacations? Paying for her expensive designer wardrobe? If you start your relationship based on high material expectations, you will constantly have to meet and exceed this high standard. My dad taught me to look more at the person than the material things. He says that a lack of finances causes divorce, and I should never be the person that marries or dates someone just for his money. I would much rather marry a guy who manages his money well and has no debt, than a guy who always spends too much to buy things he can't afford."

"Well," Malcolm retorted sarcastically, "aren't you just Miss Goodie-Two-Shoes?"

"Malcolm," Professor Christensen immediately spoke up, "you owe Allison an apology. Remember the rules of this class: we are to respect each other and maintain a positive attitude. Allison, you need to apologize as well…your point was well taken, but a little rude."

Malcolm apologized, though he sounded a little sullen. Allison was more sincere.

Justin made silent note of Allison's response about money. He decided to ask a question. "Excuse me, Professor. From what I remember of the lessons you gave, you said that we should only go into debt to acquire assets that appreciate. I understand that real estate appreciates, but why did you tell us to avoid student loans—won't a better job appreciate over time?"

"Excellent question," Professor Christensen said. "Student loans may be helpful, but first consider these points:

"One, You'll be paying interest and school will cost you more.

"Two, there are very few things that you can do to get rid of your student loan debt in a crisis. Even if you were to declare bankruptcy, your student loans debt would still be there.

"Three, it may be an unnecessary expense, as there are grants, scholarships, tuition reimbursement, and jobs that may help you completely cover your college costs.

"And four, if the economy is bad when you graduate, you may not have access to money to pay these debts. The very best you can do is delay payments, but that only increases the interest that you pay.

"Just because student loans are easy to get into does not mean they are the best thing for you. Student loans are like credit cards; fairly easy to obtain, but they come with a hefty price tag with interest and penalties."

Results of Continuously Applying to Scholarships

The bell rang. Professor Christensen dismissed the class. When Justin got back to his apartment after work, he had received a letter about a scholarship he had applied for. Justin opened the letter and read,

Dear Mr. Murray,

Congratulations! The committee has reviewed your application and has awarded a $1,000 scholarship if you are able to maintain at least a 3.3 GPA, starting with the present semester. The scholarship will be available to you at the beginning of next semester, assuming you are able to maintain credentials.

Keep up the good work! We wish you well.

Justin was taken aback. He had received another scholarship simply as a result of applying.

Tithing Pains and Blessings

On Sunday, Justin went to church. He gave his tithing on the scholarships, on the FAFSA money, and on the money he'd earned at his job. He was amazed. It was the largest tithing he ever donated at any one time in his life. He was giving hundreds of dollars. The thought did cross his mind about not tithing—after all, he was the one who had done the work.

As he thought about the amount, he remembered Professor Christensen's lesson: Paying it forward was like planting money seeds. He realized that he had been given *thousands* and that he was only asked to give *hundreds*. He gladly put the money into the envelope and went on his way.

As Justin gave his tithing, he remembered that Paul had helped him save money on books; that as he went to buy a book he just happened to be in the right place at the right time to get his job; he had been awarded a Pell Grant; he had received several scholarships; and he was enrolled in Professor Christensen's class which was teaching him how to manage his money and learn more about how to have it serve a person. Justin realized that he had been very blessed—especially at a time when his family was unable to support him. Justin had always paid his tithing but was now seeing how he had been blessed. He decided right then that he would never shortchange his tithing—it would cost him too much not to pay it.

Chapter 15: Principles and Suggestions

1. Find ways to stay out of debt: Pay for school using scholarships, grants, and jobs that offer tuition reimbursement.

2. Make relationships based on attributes, not material possessions.

3. Keep applying for financial aid and scholarships. It pays off.

Chapter 15: Warnings and What to Avoid

1. NEVER get into a relationship based on money—whether you are the one paying or the one receiving. Let relationships happen because of your personality and positive interactions with others.

2. Giving to charity, or tithing, is one of the most fulfilling things you can do with your money. If money is tight, pay your tithing first and sacrifice something else (e.g. eating out); thousands of people have stated that when they paid tithing first, unexpected money came to them.

Chapter 16
Last Hoorah for Cash

After class, Justin went up to Professor Christensen and asked about Dave and Susan's predicament—without revealing confidential information—to find out if there was anything that Professor Christensen could suggest they do. After hearing a few details, Professor Christensen replied:

"One of the things that they can do is call their credit card companies and explain their circumstances," Professor Christensen said. "Specifically ask if their credit card companies have a debt management program, one where they will lock the credit card from being used for 12 to 18 months, *and* ask if during the credit card freeze they can have zero percent (or close to zero percent) interest on the balance. Often, people with debt try to hide their problems; if they can just explain their situation, they *may* find that their credit card companies can work with them.

"Next, they need to take control of their spending. You should tell them about the prepaid debit card idea and channeling their money. This still works even for married people not in school. Specifically, they need to learn about their *bubblegum-diamond thieves* and stop them. They need to make a plan to take their extra money and put it towards their debt. I am also guessing that they are not saving. They should try to put some money towards a 401(k) plan or another retirement account. I know that it is really hard for people to save when they are in debt, but it is the habit and principle that they need to establish—while getting whatever free money they can from their employers. Additionally, as long as they can establish a pattern of savings, if they cannot pay their debts and must declare bankruptcy, generally speaking, the bankruptcy courts will not touch retirement accounts[45]—assuming that there is an established pattern of contribution (you can't just stick whatever money you have in a retirement account and then soon thereafter, declare bankruptcy). I'd recommend that they read a book called *Out of Debt, to Prosperity*.

"That should get them started," Professor Christensen said. "Getting out of debt can seem hard, but worth it. They should also make sure that they are creating ways to grow their money."

"Thank you, professor," Justin said. "I think that'll help them."

"Sure thing," Professor Christensen said as he and Justin parted.

Cars: Liabilities or Assets?

I really like this automatic finance system. Justin mused. *All of my expenses are automatically tracked—plus if I have extra money at the end of the month, I can spend it on whatever I'd like. Hmmm, I have enough for something special.*

Justin had found that there was a regional symphony concert series going on and when he called the box office, remembering his experience with his tire, he asked if they had any discounts for students. The student price was just $5 per ticket. After inquiring about the availability and performance days, Justin thought he would first ask Allison if she wanted to go. Grabbing his cell phone, he dialed her number.

"Hey Justin," Allison said in an enthusiastic voice. "What's up?"

"Hey beautiful," he began, "I was wondering if you'd like to go to the symphony with me?"

"No way! Are you serious?" Allison asked excitedly. "How'd you get tickets for that?"

"I found a way to get a discount," Justin said in a playful tone. "I haven't bought tickets yet, but I wanted to know when you were available—and if you wanted to go."

---

45 Because of the Employment Retirement Income Security Act

"Are you kidding?" She replied. "I have always wanted to go to the symphony. What days are available?"

"Thursday, Friday, and Saturday, at 7 p.m."

"I'm working Thursday and Saturday at the hotel. How about going Friday—as long as the tickets are not too expensive?"

"Nope," he replied. "I saw that I had some extra money in my monthly fluctuating expenses account. I wanted to make this something special— plus I am getting a discount on the tickets. Friday works for me."

"Oh! Thank you. Thank you." Allison said. "I'm so excited."

After ending the conversation, Justin couldn't help but think, *Yes! I love knowing that I can afford things that matter.*

Friday came. Justin ensured that his car was washed the day before. Erin came a little late to work, which put Justin in a bit of a rush. He hurried back to his apartment, changed his clothes, and went to pick up Allison.

Justin rang the doorbell, and when Allison opened the door, she looked amazing. She had a beautiful velvet gown on with her hair flowing down her back. Justin was speechless.

"Hi Justin," Allison said. "Do you like my dress?"

"You look…" Justin paused trying to capture the moment. "Absolutely stunning."

Allison smiled. "Can you believe this? I found the dress at a discount clothing store. It turns out, if you know where to look, you can find great deals lots of places. Shall we go?"

"Yes, indeed," Justin replied heartily.

As Justin and Allison were driving to the symphony, between feeling a little rushed and engaging in conversation with Allison, he didn't pay as much attention to his driving as usual.

"Aww snap," Justin exclaimed as he saw red and blue lights. Pulling into the shoulder, he waited for the officer.

"Going a little fast there aren't you?" The officer asked.

"Yes, I guess I was," Justin said. "Sorry officer. We are students from

SSU and we're headed to the symphony," Justin said hoping both the student and symphony parts would soften up the officer so he would just give them a warning and let them go.

"May I see your license and registration?" The officer asked. Justin handed both over.

The officer stepped away. Upon returning, he issued a ticket. "Maybe this will help you to remember to slow down on your way back. You can pay the $120 at the county courthouse. However, since you have no other tickets, excluding a parking ticket a few months ago, I would suggest that you inquire about paying a fine and attending traffic school—the cost will be about the same but at least that would keep the ticket off your record."

Justin felt duly chastened and at the same time annoyed. *Why do cops have to be so patronizing? I was doing so well with my money.*

Justin continued driving—this time more cautiously. The symphony was amazing, but Justin felt a little sullen. Midway through the symphony, he lightened up and enjoyed both the music and holding Allison's hand.

As they walked back to his parking stall, Justin remembered that his parking was by the hour. Now about two hours later, he would owe $10 for parking. Justin's bad mood returned.

"Justin," Allison asked. "What's wrong?"

"Oh, sorry. I was just thinking about the cop and how condescending he seemed, and then I remembered parking and paying by the hour. I mean, I know I have the money, but I was being so careful with my expenses, and I could have paid my grocery bill with the money I lost tonight."

"Justin," Allison said tentatively and with compassion in her voice. "The evening, minus the traffic ticket, was amazing. You made it perfect for me. Thank you."

"I'm glad," Justin said half-heartedly.

"Justin," Allison said in a sympathetic tone, "I'm sorry about this loss. I know it hurts and it doesn't seem fair. Do you remember the first day of class when Professor Christensen asked if the students who left class were victims or victors?"

"Yes," Justin responded, "that was when I first started to get to know you. You said something about choosing our attitude."

"Look, at one point in my parents' married life, my dad was working as a mid-level manager of a company. He made an okay living, but he was miserable. One day, the company needed to downsize and he was laid off with a severance package. At first, my dad was panic-stricken having me and my brothers and sisters to provide for. My mom simply came to my dad and told him, 'Now the world gets to see the real man that I married; but more importantly, my husband gets to see the man who he really is.' She told him to take the severance money and pick something he wanted to do with his life.

"My dad thanked my mom, got the message, and decided that he liked people and helping people look nice; he thought about it and decided he wanted to cut hair. He went to school and got to do what he loved. He learned to manage his money, and mom commented that he was never happier. My dad said once that upon reflection, getting laid off was a blessing because it allowed him to do what he really loves. Justin, you can either choose to be a victim of your circumstances or you can do something about it—either way, I believe in you and love you."

Justin smiled and said, "Thanks for the story, and I think you are right, I need to remain positive. But I think you left something out."

"What's that?" Allison asked.

"This," Justin said as he leaned over to kiss her. The kiss filled them both with butterflies and excitement, all at the same time.

"Oh, I see," said Allison with a smile.

"Thank you so much," Justin said to emphasize Allison's comment. "Thanks for helping me to shift my perspective."

"You're welcome," Allison said. "When you first came to SSU, you told me that you were scared because your dad took a pay cut and couldn't pay for college. But, then you took an active role in your life and you received more from your efforts than what you would have, had you just relied on your dad. How could you approach this situation with the same enthusiasm?"

The question made Justin think. *What could I do to resolve this situation?* The rest of the night passed with Allison and Justin enjoying each other's company.

Crunch Time—Focusing on Finances

The semester was drawing on, and right as fall break was approaching, and Professor Christensen made an announcement:

"Most of you have done really well this semester," he said. "Many of you have reported that you have controlled your expenses, amplified your income, set and achieved goals, and put systems in place to help you accomplish your goals. I want to do something for you that will greatly bless your entire time at college *AND* I am willing to back it up with a reward."

At the mention of a reward, many class members perked up—remembering that Professor Christensen gave out real money.

"I am going to offer a reward to the student who applies to the most scholarships and saves the most money during fall break week. The winner will be given $150—cash. To win, you must submit all essays and scholarship completion screenshots—so I can see there are no junk applications. All essays should be reviewed by grammarly.com. You have ten days to submit all applications and claim this reward. Class dismissed."

There was a buzz of talk from the students as they left the classroom. Justin was excited. *That $150.00 would more than pay for that ticket—plus if I win any scholarships, I could gain thousands of dollars. I am so winning that reward.*

Allison and Justin talked as they left the classroom. "With Fall break coming up," Allison reminded Justin, "I'll be at home. Why don't you spend the bulk of it applying to scholarships? I'll bet you could apply to 20–25 of them—especially using your system."

"That's a good idea," Justin replied. "But it has got to be more. I think it is time to sell my car and cut my expenses."

"Those would definitely help. It sounds like you have the beginnings of a plan," Allison commented. "Between your scholarships and cutting expenses, you just might make it."

What Can Happen When You Are Focused

While Allison is gone, why don't I apply to at least 15 scholarships in one week? This way I can do everything possible. But, first, I am going to put an ad up to sell my car.

At work, Justin pulled out a piece of paper and started brainstorming. *What could I do to get around without a car?* Justin came up with the following ideas:

- Go to local activities and events (free)
- Use Uber or Lyft for short car trips (< $30/mo.)
- Ride with another student to go home for Christmas
- Get a nice, but used, bicycle ($100 to $150, then $10/year)
- Use a student bus pass[46] ($70 for semester)
- Get a rental car as needed for road trips (unknown cost)

Justin realized that the semester was almost over and getting a bus pass wouldn't be very cost-effective. He decided that he would, for now, go to local events and budget no more than $30/month in his fluctuating expenses for Uber—this would mean planning ahead for a trip to the store. *Wow! I don't even need my car because it just sits at my house for most of the week. I will save up to buy a bicycle after Christmas when it is warmer.* Justin went to the online student ad board and posted a car-for-sale ad. He then went to the local online classified ads and placed an ad. *I'll save about $200–$300 per month not having to pay for insurance, maintenance, and gasoline—not to mention tickets*, he thought wryly. *Budgeting $30 a*

---

46 Some schools offer these for free. Check with campus student services.

month for Uber is about 10% of the cost of a car. The other items can come later.

Justin wrote "potential expenses to cut," drew a line under it, and came up with the following: "1. Check to see if a cheaper cell phone plan existed. 2. Save up to $500/semester on textbook expenses using eBay and Amazon and similar sites. 3. Save 5% on tuition, books, housing, and class fees using a 529 Education Savings Plan. 4. Use price matching on grocery items— saving about $60 to $100 per month. 5. Continue to use the automatic money system to avoid late fees and exceeding budget. 6. Check Groupon or LivingSocial for date and fun activities within my budget. 7. Save about $100/month living off campus.

He felt satisfied now that he had posted his car for sale and made a plan to reduce his expenses as much as he was able to do so—after all, he already was living in housing that was a good deal. He then drew another line and wrote: "Ways to find scholarships: 1. Contact my department— speak with Bob. 2. Contact the school scholarship department—speak with Mr. Wheatley. 3. Use Fastweb. 4. Internet-search my major and look for scholarships."

After making this plan, Justin then emailed both Bob from his department and then Mr. Wheatley asking if there were any scholarships available for freshman students in his major. *I don't have to meet with them, just learn what they know.*

Right after Justin sent the letter to Mr. Wheatley, his boss Kevin emailed him, Jon, Dan, Erin, and others and asked if anyone would like some extra hours covering for other students who would leave for fall break. *Perfect!* Justin thought. *I could use some extra hours right now.* Justin knew that he would get paid for applying to scholarships. He quickly emailed his boss Kevin and volunteered. Kevin responded and gave him 15 extra hours. *I can spend the time applying to scholarships.*

Justin really wanted to win the prize offered by Professor Christensen, not just because of the money, but he wanted to see what he could accomplish if he pushed himself. Over fall break he followed his plan to reduce expenses and apply to scholarships.

Applying to so many scholarships was monotonous. It seemed like every application was the same: "Name," "Major," "GPA," "Address," and all the other similar fields. *I am so glad that I established this system before I needed to apply to so many scholarships so quickly.* Justin didn't know if he would make it but figured that even if he got one additional $1,000 scholarship, he would be getting $40 to $60 per hour.

A student named Fred called and asked if he could see Justin's car. They arranged a time to meet.

"I'll take it," Fred said after taking a test drive. "If you'll stop by this bank ATM, I'll get cash to pay you."

"Don't you want to go inside the bank—it's just down the street?" Justin asked. "You can avoid the ATM fee."

"Don't worry about it," Fred said. "The fees are only $2.00."

Justin knew that he couldn't tell Fred how to spend his money, but Justin couldn't help thinking *Warning, bubblegum-diamond-thief in Progress! Warning, bubblegum-diamond thief!*

After Fred paid him, they went to the county clerk's office together and got the title transferred[47]. He felt relieved. He didn't have to pay for insurance, gas, maintenance, repairs, or registration fees. Justin immediately called and canceled his car insurance. What surprised him was that the insurance company told him that they would prorate the amount owed and send him a check for the unused portion. *Sweet. Extra money that I can add to my list.*

Between scholarship applications, work, and homework for some of his classes, Justin was glad that it was fall break because most of his time was consumed. However, he did take the time to play a few games of tennis to de-stress.

---

47 If you are selling a vehicle, be sure to go to the government office where titles are registered in your state. Car sellers should be personally present when transferring title. Otherwise buyers can, intentionally or not, fail to get the title transferred, potentially leading to the seller being later sued, with the car long gone, if there is a car accident.

Chapter 16: Principles and Suggestions

1. Surround yourself with people who will lift you up.

2. Cars cost money. There are other ways to get around without having to own a car in college. See Justin's plan for ideas.

3. For any parents reading this, rather than giving your students money outright, why not give your students incentive to apply to scholarships by offering them a cash reward for their efforts?

Chapter 16: Assignments

1. Make plans for how you can push yourself to save money, earn money, and apply for scholarships and other resources, and how you can use free time and breaks from school to accomplish goals (both fun goals and financial goals).

2. Complete "What Parents Can Do to Help Their Children" or "Arranging Time to Apply."

Chapter 16: Warnings and What to Avoid

1. Don't take just risks for the sake of taking risks. Instead, take calculated risks—know what is at stake and how to prevent loss.

2. Keep your worries and concerns in check. Define your fears and create a plan to overcome obstacles.

Chapter 17
Determining Your Results

Justin had spent most of his fall break applying for scholarships, seventeen of them so far, but he still didn't know if he would make it the deadline. Justin had received his paycheck on Friday. He wondered if he should pay his tithing now, or wait till after the contest. Justin decided to pay it now. *God is the best business partner I could ask for. Even if I don't win, He has already given me so much—including being in Professor Christensen's class.* Justin paid 10% of his earnings.

Justin had until Thursday to finish up for the contest deadline. "I don't know if I am going to make it," Justin emailed Allison.

"That's okay, it is not the end of the world, but at least you can have no regrets knowing that you did your best."

"Yeah, you're right," Justin replied.

What happened over the next four days was remarkable. Justin was awarded a $4,000 scholarship and a $1,500 scholarship, and still had other scholarship applications pending. One of the scholarships was one for which Justin had applied before fall break, but free money was never something to be complained about. He had more than enough to pay for two semesters of college.

"I really don't believe it," Justin said to Allison. "I mean, two weeks ago I felt like I did when I started this semester—cash-strapped—but everything really came together."

"You were so blessed, Justin," Allison replied. "It really was remarkable to see you accomplish all that you did."

"I don't think that I could have done it without you. You really encouraged me when I needed it. Thank you *so* much."

"Sure thing! You'd have done the same thing for me."

Justin and Allison continued their walk around Steed Park. "You seem pensive. What are you thinking about?" Allison asked Justin.

"I was just thinking about the class and all that we've learned."

"I know what you mean," Allison replied.

Truthfully, Justin had been thinking about an idea he'd had, but he said: "I'm going to miss this class—and seeing you three times a week."

"What!?" Allison said with a smile. "I'm sure we could arrange to see each other three times per week."

Justin smiled. "Yeah, I think we could arrange that."

Gaining a Dream—Involving Others in Your Goal

After his date with Allison, Justin called Paul. "Hey, would you like to take a trip with me?"

"Where to? When?" Paul responded.

"How about going to Chichen Itza for spring break?"

"What?! Are you serious? I don't want to leave Anna."

"I never said we wouldn't bring her along—and for that matter, I want to bring Allison," Justin responded. "You and I will have our own place, and the girls will have theirs. It will be fun."

"Great! How am I supposed to pay for two tickets and hotels?"

"You have the money for next semester's tuition, right?"

"Yeah, but if you think I am going to use that money to go to Chichen Itza, you are crazy," Paul responded.

Justin reminded Paul about the rewards credit card that he had and the upfront bonus of two round-trip tickets. Justin also explained about getting the state tax credit by first putting the money into a 529 savings plan.

"You've already got the money. The credit card requires that we spend

$2,000 within 100 days of opening the account. Guess what costs more than $2,000?"

"Tuition," Paul said, realizing where Justin was going with this idea. "I like it. I'm so doing that for spring break! Where do I get one of those credit cards?"

Justin gave the specifics on the credit card. "We can work out the rest of the details of the trip as we present the idea to the girls. I don't want to go there alone, so who better to bring than my best friend and girlfriend? I don't think it would be a good idea to invite Allison without Anna being there."

"Yeah, I know what you mean," Paul responded. "But this idea sounds awesome; I'm in as long as the girls are."

"Me, too," Justin replied.

Paul and Justin continued making plans—all the while, becoming more and more excited. After about twenty minutes, both of them agreed on their plan.

On the last week of school, Professor Christensen told the class, "Well, we have three things left. First, the contest. Some of you seemed to have forgotten about the challenge—that's okay, I hope you had a fun fall break. Others of you applied to five to eight scholarships and saved a few hundred dollars. Other class members applied to about ten scholarships and saved about a thousand dollars. However, I had a dilemma in that the top two students effectively tied. One student applied to 17 scholarships, sold a car, wrote an outstanding plan on saving money, and worked extra hours at a job."

Allison looked at Justin. He smiled sheepishly.

Professor Christensen continued, "The other student applied to 19 scholarships and wrote an outstanding paper on saving money. This student saved money by being smart with money and avoiding larger purchases, as well as including that tuition reimbursement was benefiting education."

"I had a hard time deciding who won." Professor Christensen said. "So after speaking with the university coordinator, we decided that we would offer two first place prizes of $150 each to…Justin Murray and Allison Pratt. Will you both please come forward to claim your prizes?"

Justin was astounded. *Allison didn't mention that she was heavily involved in applying to scholarships as well.* He smiled as they stood up. After accepting the awards and shaking Professor Christensen's hand, they sat down.

"The two items of business we have left are a final project; it's a surprise. The other is an invitation to come to an assembly the university is putting on, on the 14th of December. The assembly will not be part of your grade and is not required for this class, but you are welcome to come." Professor Christensen said the final project would be emailed to them later that day.

Calculating Net Worth

At work, Justin checked his email and downloaded the attachments containing the final project instructions. They were as follows:

Get a clean, white sheet of paper and on it draw a line down the center, making two columns (or use MS Excel). The right column is for future semesters if everything continues as is. The left column is for this present semester.

In the left column, write down the number of scholarships you applied for this semester and the amount of money you got in scholarships this semester; make a subtotal. Now write down your present expenses for this semester (rent, car payments, etc.), also in the right column. Subtotal both.

In the right column, write down any scholarship monies that are scheduled to come. Then write down your future expenses if things continue as they are now. Subtotal both.

Finally, subtract the expenses from the income in each column. Now you know what you get to keep both now and in the future, if things *continue as they are now. <u>Financially, at the end of the day, it's what you keep, not what you earn, that counts.</u> This is the equivalent of totaling up your net worth. If you were to sell everything you have, at present market value, and subtract any debts or any expenses, that's your net worth. I hope that your net worth, now, is in the tens-of-thousands-of-dollars range, or more.*

Calculating Contribution Worth

Now turn the paper over. This side will have no columns. We're going to describe the contributions you have made. Write down the amount of service that you've done, in hours per month, and what you did. Total up these hours. Write down the amount and percentage of money you have contributed to charitable causes. Write down the number of people with whom that you have networked during your time here. Write down the books that you have read. Write down the classes that you've taken, both through the university and privately. Write down how you've done your part at your jobs. Write down any times that you've offered a smile to someone who was down. Write down the times that you told family and friends that you love them. Write down time that you've given for anyone that you've mentored. Write down the amount of time that you have given attention to God; for example, reading sacred writings, praying, attending services, etc.

When it comes to making contributions and making a difference, at the end of the day, it's what you give away that matters. The more that you give of yourself, the more that you will have. The more love that you give away, the more that you will receive. The more that you teach others, the more that you learn for yourself. There are two things that matter when it comes to having a life of meaning. One is having the freedom you desire—part of which is control over your finances. The second, more importantly, is being contribution-minded. When you contribute, your life means more to yourself and others.

Complete both parts of the assignment. You need to email it to me by December 13th in order to receive credit.

Find Net Worth—Example of What Can Happen

Okay, let's see, Justin thought to himself. *I applied to 53 scholarships—thanks to my blitz during fall break. I got nine scholarships. Now, what were the amounts? First, a scholarship for full tuition for four years, then a $2,000 scholarship… finally the $4,000 scholarship I just received. I can't forget my Pell Grant and the small scholarships from my dad's work. Now, what's the total?*

Justin pulled out a calculator and after punching in the numbers almost dropped it. *Over $21,000 came to me in scholarships this semester?! I want to see it.* Justin then logged into his bank account at Ally, and couldn't believe it. He saw with his own eyes the money from his recent scholarship successes. The money was deposited automatically over the past week, so Justin wasn't fully aware of the total. He had over $16,000 in his high-yield account; he had originally planned on using the few thousand he had for next semester's tuition. *Now thanks to the money I saved, and my contributions to my 529 savings plan, I have enough for tuition in that account for next semester.* Justin was stunned. *That money in my account is after paying rent and food.* Justin added up all his money in his checking and 529 accounts; he was amazed at the total.

What about my expenses? Let's see, I pay my cell phone. I don't have to pay gas or insurance now that I sold my car. I'm left with food, fun, and my goals; tuition is already covered for next semester. Justin found his net worth was about $22,000.

Now on to the contribution phase of the assignment, Justin thought. *Let's see, I went singing, I went to the old folks' home with Allison, I tried to be positive most of the time, I did my job well, I became better friends with Paul, I'm dating a wonderful girl, I helped Dave and Susan, I attended church service… Oh, wow! I had no idea I had such an impact, but more importantly, look at how I have benefited. Sure, I helped others, but as I was helping them, they were helping me to be happier.* Justin continued to list things he had done to serve others. He completed the assignment and then combined it with his net worth for grading. He sat for a while and thought about how many great things were happening in his life.

Assembly Surprises

On the 14th of December, the day after he had submitted his final report to Professor Christensen via email, Allison and Justin walked, hand-in-hand, to the assembly that evening.

"What did you think of our last assignment?" Justin asked Allison.

"I thought it was amazing; I had no idea I had done so well," Allison responded. "I mean when I added up my net worth I was shocked to see how much I had earned."

"I agree," Justin said. "What surprised me, even more, was how I had grown with my relationships and by giving service to others. I just took that stuff for granted, but when I saw my own report, I was amazed at how blessed I really am."

"We really owe Professor Christensen a lot," Allison said. "Without him, we wouldn't even know about all the resources to pay for college and that we could go on a trip just for paying tuition. Chichen Itza sounds amazing; I think it will be a lot of fun. I'm glad that we get to go with Paul and Anna. I wouldn't have agreed to go if it was just you and me, but having the girls stay in one room and the guys in another really helped. It will be way more fun with a group of friends anyway."

They arrived at the assembly at 6:47 p.m. They picked up a program and found that the assembly was a graduation ceremony for Christian J. Howards. Both Allison and Justin knew the name, as he was well-known in the community for philanthropy. They entered the assembly hall and found Professor Christensen seated on the stage dressed in graduation robes.

Allison gasped with enthusiastic disbelief. "No way!" Do you really think Professor Christensen is … Christian Howards?"

Justin smiled as they took their seats. "Things are not always as they seem," he said, realizing what the professor meant from the first day of class.

At the appropriate time, the President of Syracuse State University announced that they were having a special graduation ceremony for a guest of honor. "We are pleased to announce that Christian J. Howards is being awarded two honorary doctorate degrees in business administration and entrepreneurship."

The president went on to describe that Christian J. Howards was the fifth of seven children. He had grown up in a rural town and later married Laura Osborn, the daughter of Gordon and Betty Osborn.

At the mention of the names of Laura Osborn's parents, both Allison and Justin had surprised looks on their faces. Justin had won the Gordon and Betty Osborn Scholarship, one of the most prestigious scholarships offered on the campus. *They were Professor Christensen's, or should he say Professor Howard's, wife's parents!*

"Christian J. Howards," continued the president, "has given more than 50 million dollars to the university both privately and for scholarships. With a distinguished career in real estate and business leadership, Christian has founded over twenty successful businesses that benefit both local and national communities. The university wanted to honor Mr. Howards with these honorary degrees five months ago, but he refused until we let him teach a class at the university. From what I understand, many of those class members are here tonight."

Justin smiled. He realized they had been learning from a multi-millionaire without knowing it.

The degrees and accompanying awards were presented to Professor Howards. The audience applauded. The newly doctorate-awarded Professor Howards gave a brief speech about the importance of giving back to the community and also the importance of choosing to mentor other people.

He then said, "There would be no Christian J. Howards honored tonight if it were not for my wife, Laura Howards." He thanked his wife and then said to the audience, "She has been the one behind the scenes, always there, cheering and supporting, believing in me when I didn't believe in myself. I think that she deserves applause."

Professor Howards began to clap, and the audience joined in. Laura Howards looked a little sheepish at the unexpected recognition. When the applause faded, Professor Howards said, "That isn't all." He gave a cue, and someone from off-stage brought a large bouquet of flowers, roses and calla lilies, in a glass vase, and presented them to his wife.

"This, my dear," said Professor Howards "is for all the times that you've supported me and were content with helping our family and me to succeed. Thank you. Thank you for believing in me when few did." The audience cheered again, wildly. The president concluded the ceremony and dismissed the audience.

After the ceremony, Allison and Justin went up to Professor Howards, who congratulated them both. "Well done," he said. "If things continue as they are, you should be well on your way to having financial freedom. Allison, I am so glad that you and Justin are dating, but you by yourself have done wonders. You are also on your way to becoming very rich."

"We had no idea you were Christian Howards," said Justin. "If we had known, we would have taken you more seriously from the beginning. I'm sure most people would have."

"That is exactly why I didn't say who I was. If people aren't willing to follow correct principles in a classroom, it may not matter—regardless of who teaches them. Also, I didn't want the media following me around. I will tell you, Justin and Allison, that being rich is a way to improve the world. The richer you get the more good you can do; it is both a responsibility and a privilege. You can do more to help local, national, and global economies by being rich, *and* you can have both money and freedom."

Justin desperately wanted to know if Professor Howards had helped Justin get the Gordon and Betty Osborn Scholarship at the beginning of the semester. He thought it might be impolite to ask, but his curiosity got the better of him. "Professor, did you have anything to do with me getting a scholarship at the beginning of the semester?"

Professor Howards looked as if he were trying to not crack a smile. "You're the one who deserves any credit for the scholarships you earned," the professor replied.

Allison asked Professor Howards, "Why did you pretend to be such a jerk in the first class?"

Professor Howard shrugged and said, "To get rid of people who wanted to coast. I hope you enjoyed the class."

"I've learned more than business lessons, I've learned money management, 529 savings plans, scholarships, and so much more. Thank you, Professor." Allison said.

"Also, you helped fulfill a dream of mine," Justin said. "We're going, with another couple, to Chichen Itza by paying tuition with a rewards credit card—which I have paid off. Thank you for teaching us to aim for our goals and teaching us how to achieve them."

Professor Howard smiled and then handed them each a sealed envelope with their names on the outsides and said, "Promise me you will not open these until tomorrow."

"We promise!" Allison and Justin said in unison.

"But, what is it?" Justin asked.

"This is just a *thank you* for letting me be a part of your lives," said Professor Howards.

"Well, thank you," said Justin, and with that, they shook hands and separated.

The next morning, Allison and Justin went running together. At the end of the run, they opened their envelopes from Professor Howards. The envelopes contained personalized letters thanking them for coming to the ceremony and for being a part of the class—checks for $500!

Part of Professor Howards' letter is written below:

This $500 is to be spent on someone who needs it, anonymously; no one will follow up on you, but on your integrity, use the money to help others in need. Remember, it is what you keep and what you give away that matters. Keep yourself happy by giving to others in need.

Thanks for being in the class.

—Christian Howards

Epilogue

Justin realized his three goals: he bought his property, went to Chichen Itza, and graduated free of credit card and student loan debt. Paul, Anna, Allison, and Justin had a fantastic time in Chichen Itza—at a low cost. The girls shared a room and the guys stayed in another. Between all the hiking and good local food, the trip was definitely memorable and a highlight of their lives. Justin donated the $500 that Professor Howards had given him to the scholarship fund; the school's donors matched student contributions. Justin and Paul started a business together. [For more information see *Finding College Cash: Business*.] Justin and Allison continued to date until February when he proposed on Valentine's Day. They were married in June of that year. Allison and Justin used some of their scholarship money to invest in real estate. [For information on how he got his property, see *Finding College Cash: Housing*.]

Paul proposed to Anna at Christmas of that year. Their wedding was in May. Paul learned many of the principles from Justin about finance and business. He gladly joined Justin in starting a business. After some time, Justin and Paul decided that it was best to hire a group of managers to run their company.

Tyler and Maria dated for three months but decided that things weren't working as they had hoped and went their separate ways. Tyler did not purchase a property until two years later: he had too much personal debt. Maria kept her business going.

Malcolm had to learn some hard lessons. [To understand why, see *Finding College Cash: Business*]; Dan Frederickson, Malcolm's father, made sure he did. Malcolm later became a lawyer like his father. He kept his edge, but learned to use it as a defense attorney.

Justin's mom and dad came out on top, largely due to having an emergency fund set aside and drastically cutting their expenses. Justin's dad found another job at a company that was more financially secure; it was good that he made the change because seven months after he left his old company, the company went bankrupt—it had too much bad debt. Justin taught his parents many of the things he had learned about money and automatic success.

Justin's cousin Dave and his wife Susan couldn't keep spending on debt that they never seemed to be able to reduce. They consulted with a bankruptcy attorney. Both were surprised to learn that even if they declared bankruptcy, their student loans still had to be repaid. They decided to work their way out of debt and fulfill their obligations. [For more information see: *Out of Debt, to Prosperity* by the author.] Dave later landed a job as a middle-level manager with a smaller company. He admired Justin for having the wherewithal to buy properties and start a business and wondered why Justin was able to have so much free time and fun while he himself had to work so hard to make ends meet. However, to Dave and Susan's credit, they did follow many of the principles Justin taught them and they began to prosper as they put the principles into action. They had three children.

Justin first learned to focus on finances and then he had time for all the fun he wanted. He did follow Dave's advice about taking some fun classes and took swing dance and bowling classes with Allison. Professor Howards was right: It really was just the difference that comes from simple things done slightly differently. Justin and Allison continued to buy properties and run their businesses. When Justin reached the end of his four years at college, they found a property in foreclosure, and they decided to buy it. They found a professional management company to manage the property. After all expenses were paid (mortgage, property management, repairs allowance, insurance, taxes, etc.), Justin and Allison netted $2,600 a month in profits for the spring and fall semesters and $1,400 a month in the summer. Justin began to invest in other properties. At the end of his college career, Justin was independently wealthy *and* had time to enjoy his life—thanks largely to what he had learned from Christian Howards.

Christian and Laura Howards went on to mentor others. Often, they were paid thousands of dollars per person to do it. They came to Justin and Allison's wedding reception in June. In the wedding guestbook, Christian Howards wrote, *"Remember, Justin and Allison, it is what you choose to keep and what you choose to give away that matters. Keep each other happy and give away your hearts to each other."*

Chapter 17: Assignments (Fun Ones)

1. The author would like to hear your thoughts. Please go to *www.FindingCollegeCash.com/Feedback* to share your thoughts or ideas with the author.

2. Post a review of this book on LibraryThing.com, Goodreads.com, and places books are sold. (Hint: Reuse your review for assignment 3.)

3. Consider yourself triple-dog-dared to do the following:
   a. Save $25,000 on college costs (both saving and earning money) compared to the average student at your school.
   b. Apply for 30 scholarships.
   c. Avoid consumer debt (student loans, credit cards, etc.).
   d. Find ways to have fun and save money.
   e. Post on *www.facebook.com/FindingCollegeCash* what you liked about the book and your adventures in completing these assignments. Share this post to your wall.

4. Visit *www.FindingCollegeCash.com/Coaching* for videos and coaching to help find additional resources.

5. If you liked this book, consider:
   a. Going to *www.FindingCollegeCash.com*. Here you can watch videos, order book and other resources, and more.
   b. Reading other books by the author (some are still pending publication):
      ○ *Finding College Cash*": *Business*
      ○ *Finding College Cash*": *Housing*
      ○ *Out of Debt, to Prosperity*

6. Share this book with someone you care about.

FUNDRAISERS AND DISCOUNTS

If your school, organization, company, charity, non-profit, church, or civic establishment, would like to participate in a fundraiser, please contact our fundraising department at *www.FindingCollegeCash.com/discounts*
Here are some ideas:

- Sell books and services at a markup
- Incentivize your members for donating certain amounts
- Offer free books for quotes on insurance, sales, etc.
- Make package deals

We'd love to help your organization out in any practical way we can.

COACHING

If you would like some additional help with paying for college, please go to *www.FindingCollegeCash.com/Coaching* to view available resources. Steven offers a variety of coaching options. Steven would like to help you find resources to pay for college.

"Steven C. Roberts has some great advice for students and explains how they can get through college without student loans ~ no matter what major they're taking or their grade point average. [Steven teaches what] students can do to stay debt-free and get the education they need. If you know anyone who is in college or university, or who will eventually be enrolling, you need to [listen to Steven]!"

—STEVE KOVACS, THE KOVACS PERSPECTIVE

SPEAKING REQUESTS

If you would like to have Steven come and speak to your school, business, or organization, you can see video clips, testimonials, and speaking information by going to *www.FindingCollgeCash.com/Speaking.*

"Our company is comprised of highly technical engineers and technicians; Steven captivated them for the entire presentation length with how effectively he taught the material. Steven made the topic incredibly interesting—and even fun. . . . We are working on arrangements to invite Steven back to speak to even more of our employees."

— CHANDRA MILLS, L-3 COMMUNICATIONS

Steven has been described as funny, engaging, and amazing! Some of his topics include:

- **College without Debt:** Steven will share informative and little-known ways to find resources to pay for college for both parents and students.
- **The Purpose Filled Life:** Steven will teach what it takes to have a life of meaning and impact both in a career and personally.
- **Surviving College/Surviving Work:** Steven will teach strategies to help you thrive in a changing environment.

Steven looks forward to working with you and the success of your event.

THANK-YOU'S AND ACKNOWLEDGEMENTS

A special thank-you is offered to everyone who has helped with this project. John Donne said, "No man is an island," and that can be said of this book; it would not be as successful as it is without each of you. I greatly appreciate your help, support, and feedback, which have made this book better than what it was. Many of you have lived the principles taught in this book, and I hope that you find continued success.

Editing and Proofing:	Emily Grover, Marcia Westmoreland, Angela Ivey, and Jana Roberts Master Editor: Liz Seif
Storyline Suggestions:	Keaton Butler, Tim Johnson, Jana Roberts, Brandon Schembri, and Justin Swalberg
Typesetting and Layout:	Sheenah Freitas
Cover Design:	Maggie Wright and Ari Gold
Some of the Book Reviewers:	Pam Anderson, Abbie Aullman, Jerry Bone, Melissa Bone, Kristy Burtenshaw, Chelsie Davis, Charles Dobens, Shauna Edson, Cami Evans, Nathalie Fairbanks, Alicia Fenton, Nicole Gneiting, Emily Grover, Tina H., Amy Han, Forrest Han, So-young Han, Libbey Hanson, Mel Howlett, Chaun Jacobs, Kaeden Jacobs, Tim Johnson, Christina Loud, Christian Marshall, Tiffany Marvin Carr, Charlotte McKenzie, Tiffany Miller, Katie Mortensen, Nkenna Onwuzuruoha, John Paul Brantly, Lynnette Petralia, Lauren Popp, Christy Ray, Paul Ray, Ashley Rees, Jana Roberts, Brandon Schembri, Tanya Simler, Justin Swalberg, Stephanie Theobald, Marcia Westmoreland, Jessica Wolfensberger, and many unnamed people at the SLCC Writing Center

ABOUT THE AUTHOR

Steven Roberts graduated from Brigham Young University in 2008. He received 35 scholarships and grants—including three prestigious scholarships. He also worked as both a teaching assistant and research assistant during his undergraduate studies, which were worth more money than what tuition and books cost him. Steven later said: "I was not a perfect student, but if I had known then what I know from writing this book about paying for college, I would have saved even more on college and graduated very well off."

Steven lives near Ogden, Utah and has a wonderful wife and three children. He enjoys hiking, cooking, writing, and spending time with his wife and family. He thanks his many mentors and friends who have contributed to the success of the projects he has worked on.

Made in the USA
Coppell, TX
26 January 2022

72370943R00142